Eighteenth-Century Europe 1713-1789

# Eighteenth-Century Europe
## 1713-1789

M. S. ANDERSON

OXFORD UNIVERSITY PRESS

London   Oxford   New York

OXFORD UNIVERSITY PRESS

Oxford London New York
Glasgow Toronto Melbourne Wellington
Cape Town Salisbury Ibadan Nairobi Lusaka Addis Ababa
Bombay Calcutta Madras Karachi Lahore Dacca
Kuala Lumpur Hong Kong Tokyo

First published by Oxford University Press, London, 1966
First published as an Oxford University Press paperback, 1966

This reprint, 1970

Printed in the United States of America

# Contents

# Maps

# 1
# The Map of Europe in the Early Eighteenth Century

THE PEACE SETTLEMENT of 1713–14, embodied in the treaties signed at Utrecht, Rastadt, and Baden, which ended the War of the Spanish Succession, marks an important dividing-line at least in the political history of western Europe. Yet clearly it did not begin a new epoch, as the outbreak of war in 1914 or even the Vienna peace settlement of 1815 did. The Europe of 1713 was complex and backward-looking in its political structure. Both international relations and the government and administration of the European states were still littered with the remnants of past ages. The political history of the next three generations is largely one of a struggle to cast off or modify this inheritance. Over most of western and central Europe this struggle was at least a partial failure. This is the main explanation of the potentially revolutionary mood of important social groups during the last decades of the eighteenth century.

In 1713 the circumference of Europe was occupied by relatively powerful states many of which were becoming more powerful. Its centre, on the other hand, was still, as it had been for centuries, an area of political division and weakness. In the west France, in spite of her defeats in the War of the Spanish Succession, was still clearly the greatest European state. No other possessed a population comparable with the eighteen million people ruled by Louis XIV, or an army which could challenge in size or quality the 400,000 men of whom he could dispose at the height of his power. No major continental state except Spain possessed a territory so geographically unified and easily defensible as that of France. Her economic resources, above all in fertile land, seemed almost equally impossible to match, while the loyalty of the French people to their king aroused the envy of Louis's brother-monarchs. French diplomacy was the best-organized and best-informed in Europe; by the early eighteenth century, as the unplanned and almost automatic result of France's political and military power, French had become the major diplomatic language of the western and central parts of the continent. Partly because of the enormous political influence of France, partly because of its intrinsic merits, French culture in all its forms—literature, art, architecture, even fashions and cookery—was influencing the whole of Europe and threatening to dominate completely some culturally backward areas such as Scandinavia, the German states, Poland, and later Russia.

Behind this magnificent façade there were very serious defects, some of them clearly visible by 1713. The machinery of government in France suffered from all the complexities and illogicalities which afflicted the governments of the old régime everywhere in Europe. Local and regional rights, traditional peculiarities and exemptions, made unified administration impossible. Economically the country was divided by internal tariff barriers, by innumerable tolls on roads and rivers, by the lack of any national currency or system of weights and measures. The privileges of the nobility, of the church, of the provincial estates and the *parlements* (see pp. 92–3) were as deeply entrenched as anywhere in Europe. The energy and prestige of Louis had kept these divisive and obstructive forces under reasonably effective control. But even before the end of his reign there were signs that this control might break down, and under his weaker successors this breakdown took place with immense results for France and Europe. Of more immediate importance in 1713 was the near-collapse of the French finances. Neither new taxes such as the *capitation* introduced in 1695 and the *dixième* in 1710, nor greatly increased sales of government offices, enabled the government to cope with the financial drain of Louis's wars. The French fiscal system could not tap the un-

doubted wealth of the country effectively enough to allow the
king to realize his military ambitions without ruining the
monarchy. France's financial problems, so acute in 1713, were
never solved during the eighteenth century. They were indeed
insoluble without drastic changes in the political and above all
in the social structure of the country. It is significant that
throughout this period the post of Contrôleur-Général des
Finances changed hands more frequently than any other great
office of state; in the years 1717–89 it was held by twenty-five
different persons.

The power and prestige of France had been built during the
second half of the seventeenth century in part upon the decline,
indeed the prostration, of Spain, hitherto her greatest rival. The
collapse of Spanish power, above all during the catastrophic
generation 1660–90, is a development without parallel in European history and not altogether easy to explain. The crippling
military burden imposed by the need to defend Spain's European possessions—Naples, Sicily, Milan, Sardínia, the southern
Netherlands, and the Free County of Burgundy—certainly
contributed. The overwhelming influence of the Catholic
church was certainly hostile in many ways to economic progress.
So was the mania for titles and government appointments which
diverted so much energy and capital into unproductive uses and
spread throughout Spain the mentality of the *rentier* and the
official at the expense of that of the merchant, the artisan, and
the industrialist. Currency inflation and wild fluctuations in the
value of the coinage gave the *coup de grâce* to the country's
economic life. By the early 1680s the collapse was complete.
Bankrupt, almost defenceless, her trade and much of her re-
maining industry dominated by foreigners (mainly Frenchmen
and Genoese) Spain's influence was at its nadir. During the
War of the Spanish Succession (1702–13) she and her empire
became the objects of the greed and ambition of stronger states
—France, Britain, and the Habsburg monarchy. Yet by 1713
there were signs of recovery. Although Philip V, the grandson
of Louis XIV whom the treaty of Utrecht established on the
Spanish throne, was a poor creature, at least in later life, the
war had given the Spanish monarchy an opportunity, which

## Europe in 1713

Boundary of the Empire

Prussian Territory

Habsburg Territory

DEN

POLAND

RUSSIA

Moscow

Warsaw

Kiev

Poltava

Cracow

Budapest

Black Sea

Bucharest

Sofia

Constantinople

OTTOMAN

Salonika

EMPIRE

ANEAN SEA

REGMARAD

was taken, to break down the autonomy of Aragon and above all of the intractable province of Catalonia. After 1713 the political and administrative unity of Spain was still very incomplete; but it was considerably greater than ever before. Under French influence important reforms in the central administration had been carried out. The cumbersome system of councils which had existed under the Spanish Habsburgs was largely replaced by one of government by ministries. A great French administrator, Orry, did a good deal to improve the system of taxation and more than anyone else enabled Philip to maintain himself in Spain during the war.

To politically conscious Spaniards, it is true, the settlement of 1713 seemed a disaster, for it deprived Spain of her empire in Europe. Naples, Milan, and Sardinia went to the Austrian Habsburgs, as did the Spanish Netherlands. Sicily fell to the Duke of Savoy. Worst of all Gibraltar and the island of Minorca were annexed by heretical Protestant Britain. But Spain's political power, apparently so reduced, was now more soundly based than for over a century. Freed of the incubus of her European possessions she had now the chance, if she chose to take it, to concentrate on the development of her own territory and her enormous overseas empire. She was far less exposed than before to the vagaries of international relations in Europe and the pressure of her enemies. In spite of her economic backwardness and relatively small population (about eight million) she still ranked as a great power.

Great Britain was the third of the major states which formed the western circumference of Europe, and the most rapidly developing of the three. Her population was small compared to that of France. Her military power was not impressive by the standards of a great continental state; in the first years of the century her greatest commander, the Duke of Marlborough, argued that she could not afford to maintain for any length of time armed forces totalling more than 70,000 men. She was still regarded as the most politically unstable of all the major European states. The civil wars of the seventeenth century and the revolution of 1688 marked her as rebellious and difficult to govern; and in the early eighteenth century the threat to

George I and George II offered by the Jacobites, the supporters of the Stuart king James II exiled in 1688 and his heirs, appeared to confirm this judgement. Yet by 1713 she possessed sources of strength which no other state enjoyed. In the last years of the seventeenth century she had become the greatest naval power in the world; and this naval supremacy was henceforth the most important single element in her European position. It played a great role in the expansion of her overseas trade, and hence of her whole economy, during the eighteenth century. It was the foundation of her great and growing colonial empire. Effectively used, it allowed her to attack the seaborne trade of her rivals. While she held Gibraltar and Minorca it made her a Mediterranean power. Most important of all, it safeguarded her from invasion.

The other pillar of Britain's power was her financial strength. Before the end of the seventeenth century she had evolved the great fiscal innovation of the funded debt. Henceforth the National Debt, in spite of the fears for her financial stability which its growth aroused both at home and abroad, was to be one of the foundations of her greatness. The general confidence of investors in government stock; Britain's possession of an evolving and relatively advanced banking system; the fact that her system of taxation was less rigid and inequitable than those of her rivals, all helped her to play in the affairs of Europe a role to which her size, her population, her history, and her geographical position scarcely entitled her. No state in the history of Europe has achieved so great a position with such relatively small resources in territory and population; it is not surprising that a distinct note of resentment is audible in much eighteenth-century comment on the growth of British power.

The Dutch Republic, the great naval and commercial competitor of England during much of the second half of the seventeenth century, was now in obvious decline. A cumbersome federation of seven sovereign republics, each with its own estates and administration, it had the most complex and decentralized political structure of any European state. Its disunity was increased by the enmity, potentially very acute, between the monarchical tendencies typified by the House of Orange (the family of William the Silent, the leader of the struggle for independence from Spain in the later sixteenth century) and the republican forces represented by the urban patriciate of Amsterdam, by far the greatest Dutch city. The death in 1702 of William III of Orange, who had for thirty years been General Stadholder of the federation, marked the beginning of a long period of republican rule and of a sharp decline in the international influence of the Dutch. Their economic importance, so great during much of the seventeenth century, was also being eroded. The Dutch Republic was still the greatest European centre of large-scale financial dealings; but its industry and trade were in slow but unavoidable decline, at least in relation to those of many other parts of western Europe, and its naval power was now definitely inferior to that of Britain.

In eastern, south-eastern, and east-central Europe there were also powerful states. But in many ways they had little in common with those of the west. They were more recent creations, poorer, more dominated by military considerations and necessities, and usually with very different social structures. Russia, the most important of the eastern powers, was a startling and unexpected newcomer on the stage of European politics. Until the end of the seventeenth century, in spite of an accelerating influx of European intellectual and technical influences, she had counted for little in the calculations of most European governments and for nothing in those of the great western states. That she would eventually become a great European power was certain. That she became one in the first decades of the eighteenth century was the work of her ruler Peter I (Peter the Great). The war against Sweden (hitherto the dominant Baltic power), which he began in 1700, placed Russia under intense strain for a decade. But in 1709 the destruction of a Swedish army at Poltava in the Ukraine and the flight to Turkey of its commander, Charles XII, the hitherto irresistible Swedish warrior king, shook Europe into recognition of the great new political force which was taking shape in the east. Poltava brought Peter a dominant position in Poland and great influence in north Germany and the Baltic. It made Russia the object in central and much of western Europe of an interest and even fear which she had never hitherto inspired. The Swedish Baltic empire did not collapse instantaneously as a result of Charles's defeat; the war which had begun in 1700 dragged on until 1721, accompanied by an immense amount of diplomatic activity. When peace was made in that year at Nystad in Finland, Russia received Estonia, Livonia, and part of Karelia, and thus established herself securely as a Baltic power. But by then Peter had already ranked for a decade as one of the great monarchs of Europe.

There were important limits to the strength of Russia. She was a poor, undeveloped country, desperately short of capital and skilled labour and with very inadequate internal communications. Peter's efforts to stimulate the growth of industry had had little permanent success, with the important exception of the iron and copper industries of the southern Urals. Moreover the tsar, as a more or less unplanned result of his system of military conscription and of the poll-tax he introduced in 1718, had begun an extension and consolidation of serfdom, already well established as a legal status in Russia, which was to have great and unfortunate results for the later development of the country. Even more important, Russian religious prejudices and traditions were in the early eighteenth century still extremely hostile to the growth there of western influences and to the whole idea of extending contacts with Europe. Peter's innovations—the strengthening of the army and all that it implied; the building of a navy; the introduction of European administrative methods (notably in the creation in 1718–19 of administrative colleges or committees to control the main departments of government)—were all intensely unpopular with religious conservatives. In 1718 Peter's son Alexis paid with his life for his essentially religious opposition to the tsar's policies. Nevertheless the second decade of the eighteenth century saw Russian prestige in Europe at a high level. Peter possessed a great army and a rapidly growing navy. He could negotiate on terms of equality with any ruler and in his last years, before his death in 1725, even hoped to marry his daughter to the young Louis XV. The spread of serfdom, whatever its human cost, did nothing in the short run to limit the military or political power of Russia. Religious opposition was cowed and the church successfully brought under the control of the government by the setting-up in 1721 of the Most Holy Directing Synod, Peter's creation and agent. Russia was still to most Europeans an enigma. It was still far from certain that she would maintain permanently the international position which Peter had given her. But it was already clear to acute observers that she was a state on a different scale and with quite different potentialities from those of western or central Europe.

South-eastern Europe continued to be dominated, as it had been for the last three centuries or more, by the Ottoman Empire. But this unwieldy, heterogeneous state, so mixed in race, language, and religion and covering so vast and varied a geographical area—from the Caucasus to the Yemen, from the Persian Gulf to the Adriatic—was now in decay. As recently as 1683 its armies had laid siege to Vienna. But by the end of the seventeenth century the Austrian Habsburgs had reconquered from the Turks the whole of the middle Danube valley; and in the new Austro-Turkish war which broke out in 1716 they were to capture Belgrade. When peace was made at Passarowitz in 1718 they acquired much of Serbia and part of Wallachia. It seemed that most of the Balkans might soon fall under Austrian control. Both on land and sea the armed forces of the Ottoman Empire had ceased to be the terror to its neighbours that they had been in the sixteenth century. Economically, moreover, the Ottoman Empire was increasingly weak by comparison with the other great states of Europe. Its population was probably falling. It had completely failed to develop industries organized on anything more than a rather primitive handicraft basis. In its trade with the European states it remained a mere supplier of raw materials; and this trade was almost entirely in the hands of the privileged foreign (notably French) merchants to be found in all its main ports. No ruler comparable to Peter the Great had forced the Empire to reform and strengthen itself. The privileged military corps of the janissaries, now a hereditary group of little value in war, was powerful enough to block any proposal for modernization of the army. Religious conservatism, led by the *ulema*, the Moslem priesthood which was the only educated class the Empire possessed, consistently and effectively opposed foreign innovations of any kind. It thus ensured that Turkish intellectual life remained hopelessly backward; not until 1727 did a *firman* of the Sultan Ahmad III authorize the printing of books in Turkish, though there was never any official restriction on printing in other languages. The political unity of the Empire, always hard to maintain, was increasingly threatened as the effectiveness of the central government waned. Egypt had for long been controlled by the quarrelsome Mamluks, a ruling group composed mainly of former Circassian slaves converted to Islam. The pashas of Damascus, Mosul, and Baghdad were tending to become the rulers of independent principalities, while even in Asia Minor local notables, the *derebeyis* and *ayans*, were for considerable periods able to disregard completely the orders of the sultan and the central government. Now for the first time there seemed some chance that the proposals for the partition of the Ottoman Empire between the states of Christian Europe, which had been appearing for generations in the west, might be realized. Traditionally, and still in area and population, the Empire was a great power. In fact it was now becoming a victim-state, the prey of neighbours better able to meet the challenge of changing circumstances and new opportunities.

The Habsburg monarchy, the group of territories in central Europe (Upper and Lower Austria, Styria, Carinthia, the Tyrol, Bohemia, Moravia, Silesia, the Kingdom of Hungary) ruled by the head of the Habsburg family, was also ill-adapted for growth, perhaps even for survival, in the competitive state-system of eighteenth-century Europe. The Habsburg territories were not a state at all in 1713; it is arguable that they never became one. Each of them retained its distinctive character and traditions; and these divisive forces were usually embodied in local institutions, such as the Bohemian and Hungarian diets, which retained real power and could offer real resistance to any centralizing efforts of the monarchy. In particular the Hungarians remained intensely conscious of their separate identity. It was only in 1687 that the Hungarian throne had become hereditary in the Habsburg family, and in 1703–11 a serious nationalist and anti-Habsburg revolt held much of Hungary in its grip. The

acquisition in 1713 of Milan, Naples, and the Spanish Netherlands, though a considerable military and diplomatic success,
helped to increase the disunity of the territories ruled by the
monarchy. Apart from these more fundamental factors even
the antagonism which often existed between the different organs
of the Habsburg government, to an extent hardly seen elsewhere
in Europe, was a serious obstacle to reform. Thus rivalry between
the Aulic Chamber, traditionally the main central financial
institution of the monarchy, and the Wiener Stadtbank founded
in 1724, seriously impeded fiscal reform during the last years
of the Emperor Charles VI.

Moreover the Habsburgs, more than most European dynasties, needed to be able to mobilize effectively the resources of
their territories. Since early in the fifteenth century the title of
Holy Roman Emperor, theoretically elective, had been held
without a break by members of the family. But it had long
ceased to confer on its holder any material advantage. As the
German states escaped more and more completely from the
control of the Emperor the imperial dignity became more and
more empty; it no longer provided him with either men or
money, in so far as it had ever done so. The real power of the
Habsburgs in the eighteenth century thus depended entirely on
their possession of great hereditary territories in central Europe.
But their imperial title still involved obligations. The Emperor
was still in theory the greatest secular monarch in Europe. He
had the dignity and prestige of a great office to maintain. He
was still looked to by most of the German states as their protector against attack from outside the boundaries of the Holy
Roman Empire; Leopold I during the second half of the seventeenth century had taken seriously, though with little practical
effect, his duty to defend the western frontiers of the Empire
against French aggression. Moreover the Habsburg territories
were very exposed to attack: by France on Milan or the southern
Netherlands; by the Turks on Hungary or Croatia; perhaps in
the future even by Russia on Transylvania. More than any other
monarch in Europe the Emperor needed to be militarily strong.
Yet his territories, though very extensive, were for the most part
poor and backward. Of the hereditary provinces only Bohemia

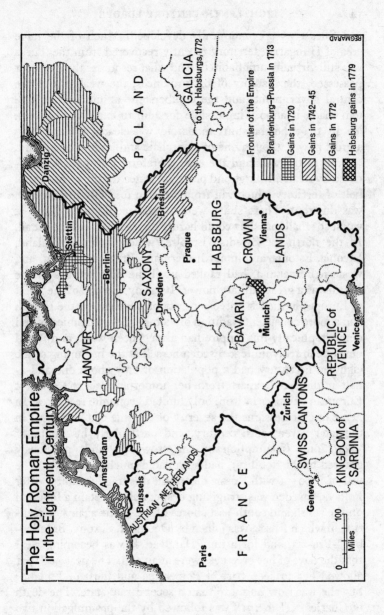

The Holy Roman Empire in the Eighteenth Century

Legend:
— Frontier of the Empire
Brandenburg–Prussia in 1713
Gains in 1720
Gains in 1742–45
Gains in 1772
Habsburg gains in 1779

POLAND

GALICIA to the Habsburgs, 1772

Danzig
Stettin
Berlin
Breslau
SAXONY
Dresden
Prague
HANOVER
HABSBURG
CROWN
Vienna
LANDS
Amsterdam
BAVARIA
Munich
AUSTRIAN NETHERLANDS
Brussels
SWISS CANTONS
Zürich
Geneva
REPUBLIC of VENICE
Venice
FRANCE
Paris
KINGDOM of SARDINIA

0   100
Miles

REGMARAD

and Silesia were economically developed. Much of the huge area of Hungarian territory recently recovered from the Turks was still virtually uninhabited. And what resources the Emperor possessed, the disunity of his provinces, the weakness of the central government, and the cumbersome administrative system made it almost impossible for him to exploit effectively. Yet by 1713 the Habsburg monarchy was clearly in many ways a great power, though one of an archaic and undeveloped kind.

Both in the west and the east, therefore, Europe was dominated by relatively large and powerful states. In the great central belt of territory which ran from Sweden to Sicily the position was different. There states were at best medium-sized and at worst so small that they could hardly be regarded as states at all. In the north the Swedish Empire, which included Finland, Livonia, Estonia, and in north Germany Bremen, Verden, and western Pomerania, had ranked until the first decades of the century as a great military power. Its army was one of the finest in Europe; in the last three generations none except the French had a more consistent tradition of victory. Yet economically and demographically this empire had always been weak, and it had never been truly united. Sweden herself at the beginning of the eighteenth century had a population of only about one-and-a-half million and, apart from her importance as the greatest European exporter of iron, only limited economic resources. In her Baltic possessions the severity of the rule of Charles XI in the later seventeenth century, and particularly his policy of 'reductions' (resumption by the crown of lands previously granted to the nobility), had stimulated much discontent. The war of 1700–21 with Russia destroyed this fragile empire. After Poltava, Sweden was struggling desperately to retain a foothold on the south and south-east shores of the Baltic against a coalition in which Russia was joined by Denmark, Saxony, Brandenburg-Prussia, and for a time Hanover. It was becoming clear that the days of her greatness were at an end. The peace of 1721 allowed her to keep part of Pomerania and most of Finland; but she was now no more than a second-rate state. The death of Charles XII in 1718 was followed by the promulgation two years later of a constitution which drastically limited the hitherto absolute powers of the Swedish monarchy. For the next half-century the political life of the country was to be little more than a series of struggles between different noble factions, backed and often paid by foreign powers, above all Russia and France. Denmark-Norway, her great Scandinavian rival, had never been more than a second-rate power. She gained little from her exertions in the Great Northern War and played in general little effective part in the international struggles of the eighteenth century.

Sweden and even Denmark-Norway were states of respectable size. But over much of Germany political division had by now been pushed to the point of atomization. The Reformation and the Thirty Years War, coupled with the influence of foreign powers, above all France, had completed the disintegration of the Holy Roman Empire which had been in progress for centuries. The larger German states—Saxony, Bavaria, Hanover, Brandenburg-Prussia, the Palatinate—could now disregard completely the authority of the Emperor when it suited them to do so. The Imperial Diet, an assembly of representatives of the German princes, continued to meet fairly regularly in Frankfurt; but it was a weak, divided body, an ineffective heritage of the imperial past. Moreover the importance of Germany in the economic life of Europe had fallen markedly, even catastrophically, during the previous two centuries. The imperial free cities of the west and south, so thriving in the later Middle Ages, were now mostly in decay (with one or two important exceptions such as Frankfurt and Hamburg). The great commercial opportunities opened to the states of western Europe by geographical discovery and the growth of colonial empires had made Germany an economic backwater. Of the more important German states it was Saxony which seemed to most contemporaries in the early eighteenth century to have the greatest political significance. She was the wealthiest and most developed of them; her court was the most luxurious in Germany and her capital, Dresden, was becoming one of the finest cities in Europe. Moreover her ruler, the Elector Frederick Augustus I, had since 1697 been King of Poland (under the title of Augustus II) and thus a figure of some importance in the politics of Europe. Bavaria, though large, was by comparison undeveloped; the Palatinate was relatively small and weak; Hanover, whose ruler was in 1714 to become King of England, had achieved the dignity of an electorate only as recently as 1692. None of these could hope to play an independent role of much significance.

Already, however, there were visible many of the forces which were to make Brandenburg-Prussia within little more than a generation by far the most powerful of the German states. The sandy plains of Brandenburg were poor and infertile; but the undeveloped Hohenzollern territories offered more scope for growth than any of the smaller states of western and central Germany. By 1713 they were scattered piecemeal from Memel to the lower Rhine; the Hohenzollerns already possessed the skeleton of a state which might eventually engulf the whole of the North German plain. Moreover the defence and expansion of these divided possessions had forced the 'Great Elector', Frederick William, before his death in 1688, to create an army crushingly large in terms of his meagre resources. He had also begun the creation of the great Prussian bureaucratic machine. This did not eliminate the influence of provincial diets and provincial particularism; as late as the end of the 1780s a very well-informed French observer could speak of Brandenburg-Prussia, with considerable exaggeration, as 'made up of ten or twelve sovereign states independent of each other'. But it henceforth bound together with increasing effectiveness the territories of the Hohenzollerns and allowed their rulers to draw with increasing efficiency upon their limited resources. Frederick I, the successor of the 'Great Elector', achieved little in a military sense though he secured the royal title for the Hohenzollern dynasty from the Emperor. Under Frederick William I, however, who succeeded to the throne in 1713, both the army and the bureaucracy were to be raised to a hitherto unknown level of size and efficiency. The Prussian state, of which they were the cornerstones, was the greatest administrative achievement of eighteenth-century Europe.

The success of the Hohenzollerns contrasts sharply and significantly with the military impotence and administrative collapse visible in Poland. The terrible decade of the 1650s had

seen her temporarily overwhelmed by a host of enemies—
Swedes, Prussians, Russians, and Ukrainian Cossacks. From
that disastrous period she had to some extent recovered; but
during the third quarter of the seventeenth century her population probably fell by over thirty per cent. Moreover the use of
the *liberum veto*, which allowed any member of the diet to
disrupt it and bring its work to a standstill, became increasingly
common during the last decades of that century. The monarchs
of Poland, themselves elected by the nobility, were now quite
powerless to check the selfishness and irresponsibility of their
creators, especially those of the great magnates of Lithuania.
These weaknesses were accentuated by the events of the early
eighteenth century. The first half of the Great Northern War
was fought largely on Polish territory and did enormous damage
to the economic life of the country; the first quarter of the
century saw another catastrophic drop of perhaps a quarter in
Poland's population. The Saxon king, Augustus II (1697–1733),
owed his position to the support of Peter the Great; it was the
Russian victory at Poltava which established him securely upon
the throne. The irresponsibility of the magnates was now such
that during his reign eight out of a total of twenty diets were
broken up by the use of the *liberum veto* and fewer than half
did any real work. With undeveloped economic resources and
small and politically powerless towns; with an army limited in
1717, by agreement between the king and magnates, to a mere
24,000 men; with no effective administration and the most
factious and selfish nobility in Europe, Poland had ceased to be
a state. She was now merely the prey of more powerful neighbours.

Italy was also an area of political weakness and division,
though here the process of fragmentation had gone much less
far than in Germany and there was nothing comparable to the
chaos which reigned in Poland. The acquisition by the Habsburgs of the Duchy of Milan and the Kingdom of Naples, the
latter the largest though in many ways the most backward of the
Italian states, made their influence for the time being dominant
in the peninsula. Of the other Italian states none was of more
than secondary importance. The Republic of Venice, with a great

history behind her, continued to enjoy some of her former reputation for efficient government. But she was now economically
and intellectually decadent, her commerce in decline, her armed
forces increasingly unable to defend her trade and territory
effectively. The Grand Duchy of Tuscany, though it included
such traditionally important cities as Florence and Siena and
possessed in Leghorn one of the great seaports of Europe, was
stagnant and parochial under the sway of its last Medici rulers.
The Papal State, misgoverned for generations, was one of the
poorest and most backward parts of Italy, and the Pope himself
more and more impotent to influence European politics. The
Duchy of Savoy, in the north-western corner of the peninsula,
was also a poor and primitive state, largely cut off from the
Mediterranean by the territories of the Republic of Genoa. Yet
it alone of the states ruled by Italian dynasties was showing some
capacity for territorial expansion, as well as an obvious appetite
for it. In the peace settlement of 1713 its ruler, Victor Amadeus
II, gained the island of Sicily, which in 1720 he was forced to
exchange for the more accessible but poorer Sardinia and the
title of king. In material resources Savoy was inferior to Naples,
Venice, or Tuscany; the importance of the role she was later
to play in Italian history was as yet difficult to discern. But the
atmosphere of weariness, of apathy and decline, which lay so
heavily on much of the rest of Italy, was less burdensome
there.

At the opening of this period then, the states of Europe varied
enormously in their strength and resources. But the distinction
between great powers and lesser states, which in the nineteenth
century became relatively clear and rigid, was still blurred and
debatable. France was clearly the greatest state of all. Spain had
for generations been regarded as a great power and even the
collapse of the later seventeenth century had not deprived her
of this status. Great Britain and Russia were more difficult to
classify; but both had, in different ways, great sources of
strength to draw upon and great potentialities. So, to a lesser
extent, had the territories of the Austrian Habsburgs. Between
these powers and the petty pseudo-states of Germany there lay
a range of medium-sized political units which in certain circum-

stances might play significant roles in European politics. Some of these, such as Sweden and the Dutch Republic, were formerly important powers now in decay. Others, such as Savoy and above all Brandenburg-Prussia, were new states now rising to a higher level of importance. But they were numerous enough to ensure that, throughout the eighteenth century, contemporaries thought of international relations in terms of a system of states which could be arranged in an unbroken spectrum of importance (though the distinction between monarchies and republics continued to be regarded as very significant for many purposes (see pp. 87–9)). The idea of the great powers as an isolated and clearly identified group lay in the future.

Most observers agreed that international relations in Europe were dominated by the balance of power. It was still possible to think to some extent in terms of localized 'inferior balances'— between Russia and her neighbours in the Baltic; between French and Habsburg influence in Germany or Italy—but more and more these were tending to become merged in a general European balance which covered the entire continent. Indeed the idea of a political and military balance was now being extended to cover the relations between the colonial powers, and above all between Britain and France in North America and the Caribbean. The argument that a balance of power overseas was a necessary ingredient of a stable balance in Europe had begun to emerge at the end of the seventeenth century. Any state which dominated America and the Caribbean, and thus Europe's colonial trade, it was increasingly argued, would inevitably become so wealthy and powerful as to threaten the political stability of Europe. The implications of this idea were strongly anti-British; it seemed particularly alarming in Paris, where the French possessions of Canada and Louisiana, and perhaps eventually much of Spanish America, appeared more and more the natural prey of the expanding British colonial empire. The concept of a colonial and commercial balance as an essential element in the European balance of power had a considerable future before it in the history of international relations. In the early eighteenth century, however, it was still in its infancy. Events outside their own continent still meant little to most

Europeans; and the age of Atlantic politics, still more that of world politics, lay in the future.

Politically, then, Europe at the beginning of this period looked back at least as much as forward. New developments such as the emergence of Russia and the growth of Brandenburg-Prussia were balanced by the survival from the past of the debris of the Holy Roman Empire, the Papal State in Italy, and the declining Ottoman Empire. Within the states, methods of government were, with few exceptions, essentially what they had been for generations. Administrators were usually untrained and the more important ones recruited overwhelmingly from the higher ranks of society. Government offices were often sold and thus liable to become a kind of personal property. Everywhere local, class, and institutional privileges and traditions, effectively supported by poor communications, impeded the centralization of government. It was within this political framework that the monarchs and governments of Europe competed with each other, and that the economic and intellectual life of Europe grew and developed during the eighteenth century.

**2**

# The Struggles between the States

## 1. 1713–40

THE QUARTER-CENTURY which followed the peace settlement of 1713–14 is a period of great complexity, even confusion, in international relations in Europe. Alliances were made and broken, shallow-rooted friendships and enmities between the powers waxed and waned, with a rapidity hard to parallel at any other time in modern history.

This extreme fluidity and lack of fixed landmarks or clear lines of development was the product of several factors. France, though inherently by far the greatest European state, was for the time being no longer the threat to the balance of power, even to the independence of much of western Europe, which she had appeared under Louis XIV. Great financial difficulties; the atmosphere of disillusionment and cynicism in which the reign of the Roi Soleil ended; the personal interests of his successor in effective power, the Duc d'Orléans who acted until his death in 1723 as regent for the young Louis XV—all meant that for some time after the Utrecht settlement France was a pacific and conservative factor in the politics of Europe. This in turn meant that, freed from the threat of dominance by her, the smaller states on her frontiers were able to pursue more independent policies. During the generation from 1680 onwards the states of western Europe had been faced by a single over-riding question—whether to accept or resist overmastering French power. The threat which Louis XIV offered to his neighbours had therefore tended to simplify international rela-

tions. The partial eclipse of France achieved by 1713 removed
this factor and made possible a new growth of complexity.

Of even greater importance was the fact that Russia and
Prussia, the states best fitted for rapid and forcible expansion,
were for the time being conservative in their attitude to international events. From 1710 onwards, with Estonia and Livonia
conquered from Sweden, the main objective of Peter the Great
was merely to force Charles XII to accept this loss and end the
Great Northern War on Russia's terms. Throughout the
tangled Baltic diplomacy of the next decade the tsar was
struggling to consolidate his hold on what he already possessed,
not to make new conquests. Though these years saw a great
and apparently threatening growth of Russian influence in
northern Germany, notably in the temporary occupation of
Mecklenburg by a Russian army after 1716, Peter's policies
were no longer in any real sense aggressive. It was the persistent
refusal of the Swedes to recognize that their Baltic empire was
lost beyond recall, and their hopes of British and Hanoverian
help in its recovery, which delayed the end of the Great Northern War for so long. The last years of Peter's reign, after the
signature of the Peace of Nystad, saw him turn away from
European affairs, conclude in 1724 a defensive treaty with the
new régime in Sweden, and look for territorial gains on his
Asian frontiers, above all in Persia. The bitter hostility to
Russia of George I of Great Britain, which had been incurred
by the occupation of Mecklenburg and the threat of Russian
support for the Jacobites, and which led to ineffective British
efforts to give diplomatic and naval support to Sweden in the
last years of the Great Northern War, was not inherited by his
son; after 1727 Anglo-Russian relations rapidly improved. None
of Peter's successors—Catherine I (1725–7), Peter II (1727–30),
Anna (1730–40), and Elizabeth (1741–62)—possessed more than
the most mediocre abilities. Under them Russia, in spite of her
immense potentialities, seemed to many observers to recede
once more to the periphery of European affairs. In 1733–5 she
imposed on Poland a king unwelcome to the majority of the
country's ruling class; and she played a role, though a rather
indirect one, in the War of the Austrian Succession of 1740–8.

But not until the 1750s did she begin consistently to act as a great power.

In Prussia Frederick William I made little use for war or territorial aggrandizement of the remarkable military-bureaucratic state he had done so much to create. It was only after long hesitation that he entered the war against Sweden in May 1715 in the hope of securing the port of Stettin. Dreams of annexing Polish Prussia and the part of Pomerania which remained in Swedish hands after 1721 attracted him. Above all he hoped to receive, on the death of their childless ruler, the duchies of Jülich and Berg in western Germany, to which he had a dynastic claim. But during his reign Prussian policy remained cautious and moderate. The potentialities of the new state which was rapidly developing in north Germany were still invisible to almost all contemporaries.

During the 1720s and 1730s, therefore, the growth of the international influence of Russia and Prussia was temporarily halted, and in the case of Russia even to some extent reversed. The problems which this growth involved, the remodelling of the balance of power which it made necessary, were temporarily in abeyance. It is above all this lack of really great issues which marks international relations during the quarter-century after the Utrecht settlement and accounts for their complexity and frequent triviality.

Nevertheless the period saw a number of significant developments. The most spectacular of these in the eyes of most contemporaries was the partial reassertion of Spanish power in Italy. One of the most important legacies of the Utrecht settlement had been a bitter antagonism between the Habsburgs and the Spanish Bourbons, who had not formally made peace with each other; and the most important cause of this bitterness was the resentment widely felt in Spain at the loss to the Habsburgs of Milan and Naples, which had for two centuries been Spanish possessions. Elizabeth Farnese, the second wife of Philip V, was an Italian, the niece of the Duke of Parma. She was extremely anxious to carve out in Italy principalities for her sons, Don Carlos and Don Philip, who had apparently no hope of succeeding to the Spanish throne because of the existence of two

elder sons of Philip by his first wife. A woman of strong character, she soon gained a remarkable ascendancy over her weak and
unbalanced husband; and her antagonism to the Habsburgs was
fanned by her chief adviser, the Abbé Giulio Alberoni, an
Italian who may have dreamed of some form of political unity
in Italy and who was certainly hostile to foreign, and particularly
German, influences there. Though he fell from power at the end
of 1719 the ambitions of Elizabeth Farnese were to prove for
two decades a source of conflict in Europe.

These ambitions were not easily realized. A Spanish invasion
of Sardinia and Sicily in 1717–18, temporarily successful, was
stultified by the annihilation of a Spanish fleet in August 1718
by the British Admiral Byng at the battle of Cape Passaro, one
of the most complete naval victories of the century. Britain and
France were as yet united in their opposition to Spanish schemes
in Italy; in 1720 they forced Philip V to make peace with the
Habsburg Emperor Charles VI by the evacuation of Sardinia
and Sicily, though he received in return a promise that Don
Carlos should inherit, when their rulers died, the Italian states
of Tuscany, Parma, and Piacenza, to be held as imperial fiefs.
This was far from satisfying Elizabeth Farnese; and in 1729,
after another brief outbreak of fighting with Britain in 1727, the
British and French governments agreed to the introduction into
Parma and Tuscany of Spanish troops as a guarantee of the
succession of the Spanish prince. Events were soon to pave the
way for a much greater Spanish success. From November 1733,
with the signature of the so-called First Family Compact, the
French and Spanish Bourbons were allies; the personal rivalries
which had divided them during the years immediately after the
Utrecht settlement (see p. 25) were now a thing of the past.
The War of the Polish Succession which broke out in that year
had in itself nothing to do with Italian problems. It was essentially a struggle between France on the one hand and Russia and
the Habsburgs on the other, after the death in February of
Augustus II of Poland, to determine who should succeed him.
In this struggle, however, the facts of geography doomed France
to defeat from the start; and her government eagerly sought in
Italy a means of striking at the Habsburgs and gaining some

compensation for the check which it had suffered in Poland. The Franco-Spanish armies, supported by the King of Sardinia, were very successful against those of the Habsburgs in 1734. When peace was made in the following year, by the Treaty of Vienna, it was therefore agreed that Naples and Sicily, which together formed by far the largest of the Italian states, should be surrendered to Don Carlos. The foundations had been laid of a Spanish Bourbon domination of southern Italy which was to last for the next century and a quarter. Habsburg influence was by no means destroyed in Italy. The Austrians retained the Duchy of Milan. In 1737, on the death of its last Medici ruler, Tuscany was handed over to Francis, Duke of Lorraine, the future husband of the Archduchess Maria Theresa, the heiress to the Habsburg lands. It became thenceforth a Habsburg possession, though from 1765 onwards with rulers of its own drawn from junior members of the family. But by 1735 the ambitions of Elizabeth Farnese, at least as far as her elder son was concerned, had been amply satisfied.

The 1730s also saw the end of another, much more tenuous and unpremeditated, part of the inheritance of Utrecht—the Anglo-French rapprochement which had followed the death of Louis XIV. This had never possessed much vitality. In France after 1715 the regent was himself the heir to the throne should the sickly Louis XV die, provided that the exclusion from the succession of Philip V of Spain, which had been one of the main provisions of the settlement of 1713, was upheld in practice. In Britain George I was anxious to prevent France from giving any support to the Jacobites, whose importance as a threat to the Hanoverian dynasty still seemed very real; and the fact that he was for a number of years on the point of war with Russia and on bad terms with the Emperor Charles VI increased his vulnerability. On both sides of the Channel personal and dynastic factors thus made for Anglo-French cooperation, notably against Spanish ambitions in Italy.

But these factors were in the nature of things short-lived, as the death of Orléans in 1723 showed all too clearly. In both London and Paris a tradition of Anglo-French rivalry was now deep-rooted. In France particularly, cooperation with Britain was always opposed by former ministers and marshals of Louis XIV such as Tessé and d'Huxelles; and it was only too easy to claim that French interests were being sacrificed to those of Britain by the selfishness of the regent and his chief adviser on foreign affairs, the Abbé (later Cardinal) Dubois. By the end of the 1720s the fragile, and to many contemporaries unnatural, Anglo-French rapprochement was tottering. After 1731, with a very able and anti-British foreign minister, Chauvelin, in power in Paris, it had ceased to exist. From 1733 onwards France was cooperating with Spain more energetically and effectively than she had ever done with Britain. By the end of the decade she was becoming involved, as the ally of Spain, in the Anglo-Spanish antagonism in the Caribbean and America which had been growing for many years.

This rivalry had a number of sources—disputes over the application of the Asiento agreement of March 1714 which seemed to have begun the opening of Spanish America to British trade and which, for that reason, was always bitterly unpopular in Madrid; constant friction over British smuggling into Spanish America and the sometimes brutal efforts of Spanish *guardacostas* to prevent it; disputes over the frontiers of the new British colony of Georgia and over the right of the British to cut logwood on the Honduras coast. Above all there was the aggressiveness of much British public opinion, summed up in the slogan 'Take and Hold', and the desire of merchant groups to open Spain's American colonies, by force if necessary, to British trade. By October 1739 the cabinet, led by Sir Robert Walpole, had been driven by popular and parliamentary clamour into war with Spain. In this struggle the Spanish government expected the active support of France; and with some reason, for French fears of British domination of the Western Hemisphere were now stronger than ever. By August 1740, after some hesitation in Paris, a French squadron was being prepared for action against Britain in the Caribbean. What prevented its use and delayed the formal outbreak of war between Britain and France until March 1744 was not any change of heart on the part of the French government but the startling invasion of Silesia in December 1740 by the young king of Prussia, Frederick II.

## 2. 1740–63

The two decades which followed were the most dynamic and important of the century in international relations, at least for western and central Europe. They are dominated by the emergence of Brandenburg-Prussia as a great or at least semi-great power at the expense of the Habsburgs, and by the vast growth of the British colonial empire at the expense of that of France. It is around these two developments that the policies of the other states of Europe in the main orientate themselves. Throughout, it is Prussia, more than any other power, which decides the pace and direction of events. Frederick II is the most dominating political figure of the period which separates Louis XIV from Napoleon.

The invasion of Silesia in December 1740 was a daring gamble but not an unreasonable one. Frederick, who had succeeded his father Frederick William I in May, had at his disposal an army of 80,000 men, in many ways the finest in Europe, and a well-filled treasury. By contrast Maria Theresa, who had inherited the Habsburg lands from her father only in October, was in a very weak position. The Austrian army had performed poorly in an unsuccessful war with the Turks in 1737–9. Many of its commanders were elderly mediocrities and in 1740 the scanty forces (about 6,000 men) stationed in Silesia possessed not a single field-gun. Moreover Maria Theresa was cripplingly short of money. The material odds, therefore, were heavily on the Prussian side, at least in the short run. Also the international situation seemed favourable to Frederick. Britain, the most important traditional ally of the Habsburgs, was at war with Spain and likely soon to be at war with France. To her, and to the Dutch Republic, the other major traditional supporter of Austria, Habsburg power was merely a weapon for use against the Bourbon states. Silesia for its own sake meant nothing to them and they were unlikely to resist its conquest by Prussia. Frederick's only real fear was of Russian intervention; and this he hoped to avert if necessary, by judicious bribery in St. Petersburg. He also expected, with much justification, that the death of the Empress Anna, which occurred in October

1740, would be followed by political confusion and paralysis. For all these reasons Silesia, one of the richest areas of central Europe and the source of a quarter of the revenues of the Habsburg government, seemed an attainable as well as a tempting prize.

The repercussions of Frederick's action were immense and rapid. Charles Albert, the Elector of Bavaria, who had claims to the entire Habsburg inheritance, took this opportunity to assert them by force. In May 1741 Spain, greedy for more Italian territory, allied with him against Maria Theresa by the Treaty of Nymphenburg. The alliance was soon joined by Saxony, whose ruler also had claims to the Habsburg heritage. Above all in the following month the French government signed an agreement with Frederick by which it committed itself to military intervention on his behalf against Maria Theresa. This meant the victory in France, after a long struggle, of military forces, led by the Maréchal de Belleisle and anxious for another round with the traditional Habsburg enemy, over the more cautious and pacific attitude represented by Cardinal Fleury, who had been chief minister of Louis XV since 1726 and was now almost ninety years old. For France the results were ultimately disastrous. She threw away in 1741 a good opportunity to cast off the now largely meaningless tradition of hostility to Austria and to concentrate her resources, under favourable circumstances, on a maritime and colonial struggle with Britain from whom she had far more to fear. She embarked upon a war which was likely to be difficult and expensive and from which, as events proved, she could hardly hope to gain much. Already in April the British government had agreed to subsidize the Austrian war effort; Anglo-Spanish and Anglo-French colonial rivalries had become merely an aspect of a great and confused European war.

This so-called War of the Austrian Succession was in fact a series of largely separate struggles—in Germany, in Italy, in the Netherlands; and overseas in North America, the Caribbean, and India. In Germany Maria Theresa held her own remarkably well against the hostile coalition which faced her in the summer of 1741. She was helped by the deep disunity of her opponents, France, Prussia, Saxony, and Bavaria, by British money and by the rather surprising effectiveness which her armies soon began to display. A Franco-Bavarian invasion of Bohemia in October was a failure; by early 1742 the Austrians had invaded Bavaria and captured Munich. In June 1743 a joint British-Austrian-Hanoverian army which had now been formed in the Netherlands defeated the French at Dettingen and an Austrian force even threatened an invasion of Alsace. But these successes against the French and Bavarians were purchased by concessions, unavoidable but humiliating, to Prussia. Only by buying off the hostility of Frederick II could victories be won in southern Germany or the Rhineland. In October 1741 Maria Theresa had accepted for the time being Frederick's occupation of Silesia in return for the suspension of operations against her by the Prussian army. In June 1742, urged on by the British government, which was anxious to free Austrian forces for use in western Europe, she ceded to him by the Treaty of Breslau almost the whole of the province. In December 1745, after a new burst of fighting with Prussia (the Second Silesian War), she repeated this concession, with the greatest reluctance, in the Treaty of Dresden. Frederick's aggression of December 1740 had thus been successful. Silesia was his, though at the cost of the bitter and lasting enmity of Maria Theresa. It was after the victories he won at Hohenfriedberg and Soor in 1745 that his subjects began to refer to him as 'the Great'. Brandenburg-Prussia had become, with startling suddenness, one of the major powers of Europe. However the Habsburg monarchy had not collapsed, as had seemed likely in 1741. Maria Theresa had been able to drive Bavaria and Saxony out of the war and in October 1745 to secure the election of her husband, Francis Stephen of Lorraine, as Holy Roman Emperor. She was thus able to continue the struggle against France in the Netherlands, and against France and Spain in Italy, until 1748.

In Italy the fortunes of war fluctuated sharply. In 1742-3 it seemed that the 'Gallispan' armies might carry all before them; and in 1745 they again won important victories. But from 1741 onwards British command of the Mediterranean made it impossible for Spain to send forces to Italy by sea, a fact of great strategic significance, while 1746, after the end of the war in Germany, saw the Austrian armies gain considerable successes. Equally important was the fact that in September 1743 the King of Sardinia, Charles Emmanuel III, who had hitherto balanced between the two sides, was won over to the Austrian one by the promise of part of the Duchy of Milan. In Italy, therefore, the War of the Austrian Succession, in spite of much diplomatic activity and some very bitter fighting, ended in stalemate.

In the Netherlands on the other hand the last years of the struggle saw France win a series of great victories—with the exception of the Prussian conquest of Silesia, the one clear-cut military success achieved by any of the belligerents. At Fontenoy, Raucoux, and Lawfeldt the Maréchal de Saxe defeated a composite British-Austrian-Dutch army. By the spring of 1748, with the Austrian Netherlands in his hands, he was threatening the conquest of the Dutch Republic, which was plainly in no condition to defend itself. It was these French triumphs which convinced the British government that peace must be made; the war must be ended before the Dutch provinces had been overrun and their ports and shipping had fallen under French control. Moreover Saxe's victories more than offset what successes Britain had won in the fourth main sphere of conflict—the high seas and the colonial areas of North America, the Caribbean, and India. These successes were disappointingly small from the British point of view. It was not until 1747 that important victories were won over the French fleet and an effective blockade of the major French ports established. The French fortress of Louisbourg, on Cape Breton Island at the mouth of the St. Lawrence, the greatest fortified position on the American continent, had been taken in June 1745; but French Canada was never seriously threatened. In India the British East India Company, faced by the energy and organizing ability of J.-F. Dupleix, the Commandant-Général of its French rival, had a hard struggle to hold its own. In September 1746 Madras, one of the most important of its trading-posts, fell to French attack.

France was therefore in a strong position when peace negotiations began at Aix-la-Chapelle early in 1748. But it was not as strong as it seemed. Her finances were in disorder; the war had more than nullified the modest but real improvement in them achieved during the 1730s. The fact that an army of Russian auxiliary troops, hired with British money, was now slowly marching across Germany towards the Netherlands threatened a prolongation of the war. Louis XV himself was strongly in favour of peace even at the cost of considerable concessions; as early as 1745 he had begun to make indirect approaches to Vienna. The result was that the peace treaty signed by Britain and France in October gave the French almost nothing. Louisbourg was returned to France and Madras to the British East India Company, while in Europe the position of the two belligerents was unchanged. Since Spain could not continue the struggle without French support and Maria Theresa was dependent upon British subsidies, the Anglo-French agreement forced the other belligerents to stop fighting. Neither was satisfied with the terms it had to accept. Spain had to agree to renew the hated Asiento treaty with Britain, though only until 1752. Far more important, Maria Theresa had to accept a clause in the peace treaty which guaranteed, though in ambiguous terms, the possession of Silesia by Frederick II—a bitter pill indeed for her to swallow. Charles Emmanuel of Sardinia retained the slice of the Milanese promised him in 1743; apart from the Prussian conquest of Silesia this was the one significant territorial change in Europe after more than seven years of confused warfare.

The war had been above all a victory for Prussia. But it had also done much to strengthen the Habsburg territories, which in 1748 were better organized and militarily more powerful, and therefore more self-confident and self-assertive, than they had been in 1740. The Empress and her ministers, unflinchingly hostile to Prussia, saw clearly that Britain and the Dutch were useless as sources of active support against her enemy. In 1742 and 1745 British pressure had forced Maria Theresa to cede Silesia to Frederick II. In 1748 British diplomacy had helped to insert in the peace treaty the hated guarantee of Prussian ownership of the province. The Dutch were now at best a

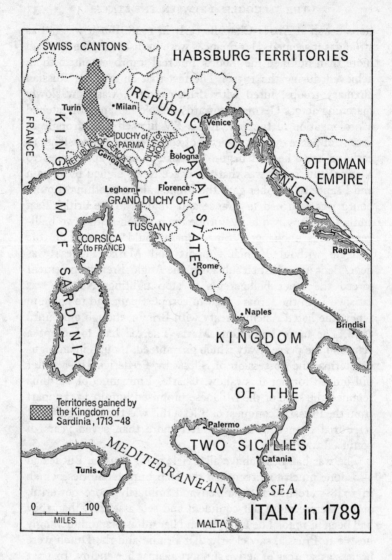

SWISS CANTONS

HABSBURG TERRITORIES

REPUBLIC OF VENICE

FRANCE

Turin • Milan

DUCHY of PARMA

DUCHY of MODENA

Bologna

Venice

OTTOMAN EMPIRE

KINGDOM OF SARDINIA

REPUBLIC OF GENOA

Genoa

Leghorn • • Florence

PAPAL STATES

GRAND DUCHY OF TUSCANY

Ragusa

CORSICA (to FRANCE)

Rome

• Naples

Brindisi

KINGDOM

Territories gained by the Kingdom of Sardinia, 1713–48

OF THE

TWO SICILIES

• Palermo

MEDITERRANEAN

Tunis •

• Catania

SEA

0          100
MILES

ITALY in 1789

MALTA

second-rate power, a liability rather than an asset to any ally. In 1745 and 1748 the Empress had already made it clear to the French government that she was willing, under suitable conditions, to abandon her alliance with Britain. From 1749 onwards, under the growing influence of Count (later Prince) von Kaunitz-Rietberg, who became chancellor in 1753, the government in Vienna was increasingly attracted by the idea of isolating Prussia by means of an agreement with France, and then crushing her with Russian and perhaps French help. An Austro-French rapprochement of this kind was not a totally unprecedented idea. Louis XIV at the end of his life had seen that the traditional Bourbon-Habsburg antagonism was now largely meaningless; and Louis XV was personally favourable to better relations with Austria. But it was not until the summer of 1755 that serious discussions between the two governments got under way. By then an undeclared war was raging between British and French forces in the Ohio valley, the two East India Companies were struggling for supremacy in South India, and the British navy was seizing French merchantmen by the score on the high seas.

These Austro-French negotiations were given a new impetus by the signature, in January 1756, of the Anglo-Prussian Convention of Westminster. Frederick II made this agreement, not from a desire to betray his French ally, but simply through fear. He knew that he was hated in St. Petersburg as well as in Vienna, and his growing uneasiness was brought to a head by an Anglo-Russian convention of September 1755 which he rightly regarded as directed against him. This association of Britain with his enemies seemed very menacing. He therefore attempted to escape from it by the agreement of January 1756, which provided for the neutralization of Germany in the Anglo-French war which was clearly on the verge of breaking out.

The terms of the Convention of Westminster did not threaten France. On the contrary it was in her interest to avoid involvement in Germany and concentrate her resources on the maritime and colonial struggle with Britain. Moreover Frederick had deliberately excluded the Netherlands from the scope of the convention and thus left it open to France to put pressure on

Britain, if necessary, by occupying them. But at Versailles there was bitter resentment of the way in which he, an upstart among the great monarchs of Europe, had dared to make a secret and independent agreement with the most bitter enemy of France. The French government, which had been making dilatory preparations to renew the Franco-Prussian alliance which dated from 1741, felt duped and humiliated. Austrian proposals now found a warmer welcome than ever before; and on 1 May 1756 France and Austria signed a defensive alliance, the First Treaty of Versailles. The Bourbon-Habsburg antagonism, which for two centuries and a half had provided the most important and permanent thread in the fabric of European diplomacy, had now been at least temporarily pushed into the background.

This did not mean that France had been won for the great anti-Prussian coalition of which Kaunitz dreamed. This was now to be created, however, not by the diplomatic skill of the Austrian chancellor but by the nervous rashness of Frederick II. The Convention of Westminster had proved a disappointment to the King of Prussia. In particular the hostility of the Russian government had not been assuaged by it as he had hoped. British influence at St. Petersburg, which Frederick had believed might safeguard him against attack on his eastern frontier, declined rapidly; by the spring of 1756 the Russo-Austrian negotiations for a joint attack on Prussia, which had been in progress since 1753, were showing signs of bearing fruit. At the end of August therefore, Frederick, convinced that his only chance was to strike before his opponents were ready, launched the most famous preventive war in European history by an invasion of Saxony which was meant to pave the way for that of Bohemia. The months which followed saw the creation of the great hostile coalition which he had wished above all to prevent. At the end of the year Russia joined the Austro-French alliance of 1 May. In January 1757 many of the smaller states of the Holy Roman Empire agreed to provide armed forces for use against Prussia; and in March Sweden joined Frederick's enemies. Above all on 1 May 1757, by the Second Treaty of Versailles, France agreed to maintain large forces in Germany for use against Prussia and to pay Maria Theresa a substantial subsidy. She thus, even more disastrously than in 1741, committed herself to expensive intervention in a war in which her real interests were hardly involved and from which she could hope to gain little. A few days later Austria and Russia signed an alliance against Prussia.

To set against these apparently overwhelming odds Frederick had nothing but the excellence of his army and administration, his own qualities of leadership, his ability to levy contributions in Saxony (from which he extorted fifty-five million guilders during the war), and from 1758 onwards British subsidies. On several occasions during the Seven Years War (1756–63) it seemed that he must be overwhelmed. In the summer and autumn of 1757—when he had been driven out of Bohemia, Hanover had been overrun by the French and East Prussia by the Russians, and Berlin was momentarily occupied by the Austrians—his position seemed quite hopeless. Again after the terrible defeat which the Russians inflicted on him at Kunersdorf in August 1759 he for a time despaired; and by 1761 he was more and more aware that he could not continue the struggle for much longer.

Yet in spite of defeats, in spite of her poverty and the loss of much of the fine army with which she had begun the war, Prussia survived. She did so for negative rather than positive reasons: because of the weakness and divisions of her opponents rather than her own strength. The anti-Prussian alliance was no more united or effective than any other coalition of the seventeenth and eighteenth centuries. Neither the Swedes nor the army raised by the small states of Germany played any effective role in the war; while in March 1758, by the Third Treaty of Versailles, the French government considerably reduced the military and financial help which it had promised to Maria Theresa ten months earlier. Franco-Russian relations remained strikingly bad, since effective action by Russia against Frederick II was impossible unless she controlled Poland, and this would inevitably mean the weakening or destruction of what remained of the traditional French influence there. More important, neither the Russian nor the French armies proved as effective as had been expected. Though they fought well and

won some great victories, the Russians never fully pressed
home their advantages to destroy Prussia as an independent
state, as they could have done. This timidity, which more than
once saved Frederick, notably perhaps in 1761, was partly the
result of the extreme caution and unimaginativeness of the
Russian commanders. It was also inspired by the knowledge that
the Empress Elizabeth was unlikely to live long and that her
death would be followed by a drastic change of policy in St.
Petersburg since her heir, the Grand Duke Peter, was well
known as a violent Prussophil. The French, for their part, were
humiliatingly beaten by Frederick at Rossbach in November
1757 and thereafter held in check in Westphalia by an Anglo-
German army commanded by Prince Ferdinand of Brunswick.
Not until the end of 1758, when the Duc de Choiseul became
chief minister, did France's war effort acquire some vigour and
effective leadership; and Choiseul was interested in the struggle
with Britain far more than in that with Prussia. Finally Frederick was saved, at the lowest ebb of his fortunes, by mere chance.
On 5 January 1762 Elizabeth of Russia died. In May the Grand
Duke Peter, now Peter III, withdrew from the war and evacu-
ated Prussian territory. With Austria exhausted and France
deeply anxious for peace Prussia's survival was assured. The
treaty of Hubertusburg, which ended the Austro-Prussian
struggle in Germany in February 1763, confirmed Frederick in
possession of Silesia. The efforts of Kaunitz and Maria Theresa
had failed.

The Anglo-French colonial and maritime war which had
begun in 1755 contrasts strikingly with the conflict in Germany.
While Prussia and Austria exhausted themselves in struggles for
a German province Britain established herself with relative ease
as the first true world power. The early years of the war were
not easy for her. Her great Mediterranean base of Minorca
fell to French attack in May 1756 and there seemed a real
danger of French invasion, the threat above all others which
terrified any eighteenth-century British government. But soon,
under the leadership of the great war cabinet dominated by the
elder William Pitt, which was formed in June 1757, the tide of
victory began to flow strongly in Britain's favour. British

dominance at sea was complete after victories at Lagos and Quiberon Bay in 1759; and while she controlled the seas Britain was immune from French invasion (which Choiseul was seriously contemplating in that year). She was also able to prevent France from sending to India or the Western Hemisphere more than a small fraction of her greatly superior military strength; only two French expeditionary forces of any size were sent overseas during the war. Cut off from the motherland and subjected to vigorous attack, French bases and colonies fell into the hands of the British with unprecedented speed. In North America considerable successes in the Ohio valley in 1758 were followed by the fall of Quebec in September 1759, the product of efficient organization and determined leadership. With the surrender of Montreal in September 1760 French power in Canada had come to an end. In the West Indies, whose production of tropical commodities, above all of sugar, made them the most immediately valuable of all colonial prizes in the eighteenth century, most of the French islands were taken in two spasms of activity in 1759 and 1762. In 1757 the British East India Company, its forces brilliantly led by Robert Clive, began the conquest of Bengal with its victory at Plassey over a local ruler. This placed at its disposal one of the wealthiest parts of India; and this in its turn, combined with British control of the seas, gave it the resources needed to crush its French rival further south in the Carnatic, the main centre of direct Anglo-French conflict. With the defeat of the French commander, Lally-Tollendal, at Wandewash in January 1760, the dream of a French empire in India had been destroyed, as it proved for ever.

These unprecedented successes gave reality to the now widespread fear that Britain might soon dominate the entire overseas trade of Europe and make herself the only colonial power of any significance. This fear found a response above all in Madrid, where British dominance of North America and the Caribbean seemed to threaten, in no very distant future, the continuance of Spanish power in South America. Choiseul, who hoped, by involving Spain in the war, to improve France's desperate position and reduce the losses she must inevitably suffer when peace was made, did his best to stimulate such fears. By 1761 Charles III of Spain was anxious for alliance with France against Britain. Such an alliance was made in August; and in January of the following year the British government declared war on Spain. The Spaniards did little to help France. Their effort to realize a recurring Spanish dream, the conquest of Portugal, was a failure. Havana, the greatest naval base in the world outside Europe, fell to British attack. So did Manila, the capital of the Philippines, which was taken by an expeditionary force from India. Britain's new status as a world power was now unmistakable.

The peace settlement of 1763 did not, as Pitt and other Francophobes had hoped, destroy France as a colonial and maritime power. Partly through the weakness of the Earl of Bute and the Duke of Bedford, who controlled the negotiations on the British side (Pitt had resigned in October 1761), she was allowed to keep the most commercially valuable of her overseas possessions. She was left with most of her West Indian islands, her trading stations in India, and, most bitterly contested of all, a share in the great Newfoundland cod fishery which provided the livelihood of so many fine seamen. The result was that the generation which followed the war saw an extraordinary development of French colonial trade, especially with the Caribbean, and a golden age for ports such as Nantes and Bordeaux. But all France's colonies of settlement were lost. Canada and the vast and poorly-defined territories which she claimed east of the Mississippi were ceded to Britain. Louisiana was handed over to Spain as some consolation for her defeats and because Charles III strongly objected to the establishment of the British on the Gulf of Mexico. These losses, though this was not clear at the time, ended for a century or more any prospect of France's becoming a genuine world power. Her empire might still be a source of wealth; but it could not be based, as that of Britain increasingly was, on the settlement overseas of large numbers of colonists from the mother country. Henceforth, even when the power of Napoleon I was at its height, France could not be more than the greatest of European states.

Spain for her part abandoned her claim to a share in the Newfoundland fishery, grudgingly recognized the right of the British to cut logwood in Honduras, and ceded Florida to Britain in exchange for Havana.

## 3. 1763–89

The peace of 1763 proved more lasting than that of 1748; but few contemporaries expected it to be permanent. Austrian resentment at the loss of Silesia, though somewhat dulled by time and the experience of the Seven Years War, was still strong. In France bitterness over her humiliating colonial losses was deep, and Choiseul soon showed that he was determined to reassert French power. The navy was rebuilt; a number of army reforms were carried out; and in 1768–9 the island of Corsica was acquired by purchase from its Genoese overlords and an independence movement there suppressed. The international events of the generation after 1763, however, differed in two important ways from those of the 1740s and 1750s. In the first place the connexion between events in Europe and those in the colonial world was much looser than during the War of the Austrian Succession and the Seven Years War. The Anglo-French struggles of 1744–8 and 1755–63 had coincided with great European military conflicts; France's involvement in these had been one reason, though not the most important one, for her lack of success overseas. After 1763, by contrast, the affairs of the Atlantic world and those of continental Europe were much more indirectly connected. Anglo-French colonial rivalries had nothing to do with the First Partition of Poland in 1772 or the great Russo-Turkish struggle of 1768–74. The War of the American Revolution of 1775–83 was little affected by the relatively unimportant War of the Bavarian Succession fought by Austria and Prussia in 1778–9. Britain from the middle 1760s to the end of the 1780s was more isolated from the main stream of political events in Europe than at any time for nearly a century.

The second new factor which marked the decades after the Treaties of Paris and Hubertusburg was the hitherto unprecedented importance of east European problems: those of the

Ottoman Empire, and above all of Poland, and the striking rise in the power and prestige of Russia which resulted from this.

The complete military and political helplessness of Poland had become clearer than ever during the Seven Years War; and from the beginning of her reign Catherine II of Russia, who deposed and succeeded her unbalanced husband, Peter III, in June 1762, was determined to assert her influence there. In April 1764 she signed with Frederick II a defensive agreement designed to maintain the existing consitution in Poland and to secure the election to the throne of her former lover, Stanis-laus Poniatowski. Already one or two Russian statesmen were beginning to urge that Russia should strengthen her western frontier by the seizure of Polish territory. As yet, however, this was very much a minority view: Count Panin, the Russian foreign minister, thought of Poland as an important member of the great anti-Bourbon alliance which he hoped to create in northern Europe during the 1760s, and wished to strengthen rather than weaken her. The roots of the First Partition of Poland lay not in Russian greed but in the international stresses set up by the Russo-Turkish war which broke out in September 1768.

Hostility between Russia and the Ottoman Empire was of long standing. They had been at war in 1736-9 and on bad terms ever since. By the later 1760s the Turkish government was deeply worried and angered by the growing Russian domin-ance of Poland; and this feeling was encouraged by the French government, which resented the obvious decline of its former influence in Poland and its replacement by that of Russia. When in July 1768 irregular forces in Russian service pursued a group of anti-Russian Poles on to Turkish territory and burnt a small town there the Turks replied with a declaration of war. The next three years saw an almost unbroken series of Russian successes. By 1770 the Danubian principalities of Moldavia and Wallachia, under Turkish suzerainty since the fourteenth century, had been conquered. In the following year the Crimea, also a Turkish vassal-state, was overrun. Most striking of all, in 1769-70 a Russian fleet, with considerable help from Britain, sailed from the Baltic round western Europe to the eastern

Mediterranean, where it annihilated a large Turkish naval force at Chesmé, on the coast of Asia Minor.

These victories could not but arouse uneasiness elsewhere in Europe. Austria in particular by the early months of 1771 was deeply alarmed at the prospect of Russian domination of Moldavia and Wallachia, since this would give Catherine II control of the lower course of the Danube, potentially the most important commercial artery of the Habsburg territories. Early in July, by a secret convention signed in Constantinople, the Austrian government promised—in return for a large subsidy and some territory in western Wallachia—to support by diplomatic means the maintenance of the integrity of the Ottoman Empire. Though there was probably little real danger of an Austro-Russian war Catherine II could not now realize, in the face of Austrian opposition, all her war aims in the Near East. In particular it would clearly be very difficult for her to retain control of the Danubian principalities. Already, however, it was becoming obvious that territorial ambitions which could not be given free rein in the Balkans were likely to be satisfied instead at the expense of Poland, which was in complete chaos, helpless to resist her great neighbours, and without any effective protector.

Frederick II, who was very anxious to avert any danger of an Austro-Russian war in which he was certain to become involved, had always wished to annex western (Polish) Prussia. As early as 1769 he put out feelers in St. Petersburg for a partition. Early in 1771 Catherine II, abandoning the policy she had hitherto pursued of maintaining Poland intact as a Russian vassal-state, showed that she was now ready to accept the idea. By the end of October Frederick had brought the Austrians also to agree; and in August 1772 Maria Theresa, with great reluctance, accepted the partition treaty which had been drawn up some months earlier. Of the three partitioning powers Russia gained most in extent of territory and could claim that the great areas she seized in White Russia had a population closely akin to her own in language and religion. Economically Austria gained most; she annexed the province of Galicia which possessed, among other resources, the greatest salt-mines in

Europe. Militarily and strategically Prussia, which more than any other power had inspired the partition, was the main beneficiary. Her acquisition of West Prussia meant that East (Ducal) Prussia was for the first time linked geographically with the main body of the Hohenzollern dominions. The partition was not altogether unexpected; suggestions for the spoliation of the decadent Polish republic had been put forward from the 1650s onwards. But commentators such as the British writer and politician Edmund Burke were right in seeing in it an unprecedentedly ruthless expression of the aggressive and competitive attitudes which underlay international relations. In this sense it was a bad omen for the political future of Europe.

It was not until July 1774 that Russia was able to force the Porte to make peace by the treaty of Kutchuk-Kainardji. The last years of the war with Turkey were difficult for Catherine II. She was alarmed by the great peasant revolt led by Emilian Pugachev which broke out in the late summer of 1773 and for two years dominated all south-east Russia. Even more serious, in August 1772 Gustavus III, by an almost bloodless coup d'état, restored the powers of the Swedish monarchy which had been largely in abeyance since 1720. This was a decisive blow to the hitherto great Russian influence in Sweden and the worst political defeat suffered by Catherine during the whole of her reign. It seemed for some months that it would be followed by a new Russo-Swedish war; this was avoided, partly because Russia's preoccupations in the Near East made it impossible for her to take the offensive in the Baltic.

Nevertheless the Treaty of Kutchuk-Kainardji, which opened the Eastern Question in its classical nineteenth-century form, was well worth the effort required to impose it on the Turks. Russia secured for the first time a direct though geographically limited outlet to the Black Sea, between the mouths of the Bug and the Dnieper. She obtained freedom of navigation for her ships on that sea (jealously guarded for the last two centuries by the Porte as a Turkish preserve) and freedom for her merchantmen to pass through the Bosphorus and Dardanelles. Above all the Khanate of the Crimea, which covered a large area of the Black Sea steppe, became an independent state. This was

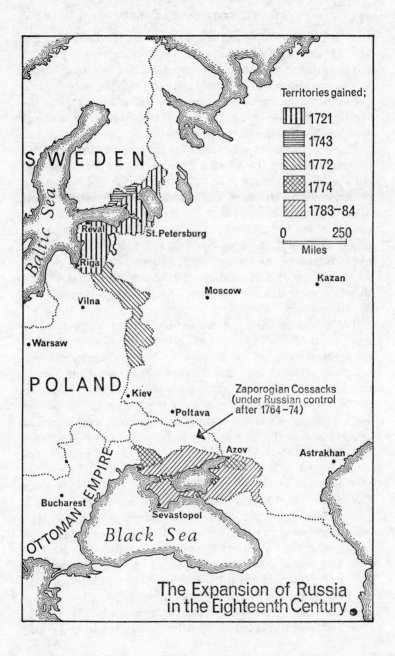

Territories gained;

||||| 1721

═══ 1743

⫽⫽⫽ 1772

⊠⊠⊠ 1774

⫽⫽⫽ 1783–84

0        250

Miles

SWEDEN

Baltic Sea

Reval

Riga

Vilna

Warsaw

POLAND

St.Petersburg

Moscow

Kazan

Kiev

Poltava

Zaporogian Cossacks
(under Russian control
after 1764–74)

Azov

Astrakhan

OTTOMAN EMPIRE

Bucharest

Sevastopol

Black Sea

The Expansion of Russia
in the Eighteenth Century

seen in Constantinople as the prelude to its inevitable annexation by Catherine II, which duly took place in 1783 to the
accompaniment of bitter but impotent Turkish resentment.
Russia was now securely established as a Black Sea power, while
her influence in the Caucasus and the Balkans was rapidly increasing. She was now, in the eyes of many observers, a threat
to the very existence of the Ottoman Empire.

These great events in eastern Europe were very little affected
by the policies of the western powers. France was unable to
aid her former protégés, the Poles and the Turks, against the
dangers which threatened them. Indeed an increasing current
of feeling in Paris urged that she should cut her losses in the
east, abandon her traditional policy of support for Poland, the
Ottoman Empire, and even Sweden, and concentrate upon her
maritime and colonial rivalry with Britain. The British government, for its part, was unwilling to take any initiative in eastern
Europe, especially since it was now faced by a great crisis in its
North American colonies.

The causes of the American Revolution can be passed over
lightly here. British efforts after 1763 to raise a more adequate
government revenue by taxation in North America aroused
much resentment there. Attempts to make the royal administration in the colonies, and particularly the collection of customs
duties, more efficient, were equally unpopular. Conflicts over
the respective powers of royal governors and elected colonial
assemblies had for long been a fertile source of bad feeling;
while the efforts of the British government to prevent un-
controlled westward expansion by the colonists at the expense
of the Indians, and to put the Catholic church in French
Canada on a more secure footing by the Quebec Act of 1774,
antagonized important sections of American opinion. The
colonial nationalism which underlay all these issues, the growing
feeling, above all in New England, that America was different
from Europe and in some ways superior to it, probably made any
lasting settlement impossible—although it seems clear that until
the later 1770s only a minority, and probably a small one, of the
colonists actually desired political independence. The idea of
Dominion status, in modern eyes the obvious solution, was still

unknown and almost inconceivable to both sides, though the
Conciliatory Propositions put forward by the British government in 1778 in a last and unsuccessful effort to mend the
breach would have given the colonists something approaching
it. By 1775, as defiance on the one side and repression on the
other mounted to a climax, armed rebellion broke out in New
England. In July 1776 the representatives of the mainland
colonies, meeting at Philadelphia, declared them independent
of the British crown.

The immediate significance of the struggle in America, and
of the domestic difficulties which accompanied it in Britain,
was the chance which they gave to France to take revenge for
the defeats of the Seven Years War. Choiseul had fallen from
power in December 1770. But a good deal of the energy which
he had imparted to French policy survived him. From the
spring of 1776 onwards the French government gave underhand
aid to the colonists; in the first two years of the war about nine-
tenths of the gunpowder they used was imported, mainly from
France. In June 1778, encouraged by the surrender of a British
army at Saratoga, which showed that the Americans would be
very hard to subdue, it entered the war. In June 1779 Spain
rather reluctantly followed the French example. Finally in
December 1780 the British government declared war on the
Dutch Republic. It took this step, a daring one in the circumstances, because the Dutch had for long been trading with the
rebellious colonies and because they had just joined the Armed
Neutrality, a league of neutral states formed under the leadership of Catherine II and intended to resist the high-handed
exercise by Britain of her 'maritime rights', particularly that of
searching neutral ships for contraband.

Against this powerful coalition Britain fared surprisingly well
in view of the poorness of much of her political and military
leadership. Gibraltar withstood a great siege by Franco-Spanish
forces in 1779–82. A temporarily acute danger of French invasion in 1779 came to nothing; and by the end of the war British
supremacy at sea had been reasserted. Though Minorca and
several islands in the Caribbean were lost, resurgent French
ambitions in India were frustrated. Moreover Britain profited

considerably, especially during the peace negotiations of 1782–3, from the disunity of her opponents. The American colonists were not anxious to exchange British rule for French domination, and showed it by signing a separate peace treaty with Britain in September 1782. Equally important, the Bourbon powers were not united. The French government wished to reduce the dangerous power of Britain at sea and to strike at her inflated prestige; but it did not, except to some extent in the West Indies and India, desire territorial gains for their own sake. Charles III and his ministers, on the other hand, had entered the war above all to recover Gibraltar. Unlike their French ally they had no sympathy whatever for the idea of American independence, which they refused to recognize until after the struggle had ended; and in 1780 they negotiated seriously with the British government for a separate peace.

It was largely this disunity of her great European opponents which allowed Britain to escape relatively lightly when peace was made with France and Spain by the Treaty of Versailles in September 1783. The thirteen mainland colonies in America were lost beyond hope of recovery; the surrender of a British army at Yorktown in October 1781 had made their independence an accomplished fact. Minorca and Florida, moreover, had to be ceded to Spain; one or two West Indian islands and West African trading-posts to France. But Canada was retained. So was Gibraltar, in spite of the most intense efforts by Spain to recover it; and the war years saw an important consolidation of British power in India. The one constructive result of the struggle was the creation of a new and independent (though as yet very disunited) state in North America—the first great victory for colonial nationalism and the birth of what some contemporaries already saw as a potential world power. American independence was a very serious defeat for Britain; unfriendly observers such as Frederick II concluded that the days of her greatness were over. But none of the real bases of her strength had been undermined. Her navy remained the greatest in the world. Her trade with the American colonies was more valuable after they had gained their independence than before. The Industrial Revolution (see pp. 68–71) was now beginning to give her a clear and qualitative economic superiority to all the rest of Europe. A commercial treaty of 1786, which opened the French market for the first time to many types of British manufactured goods, showed that in industrial efficiency she was now drawing far ahead of her great rival. For Spain the war had been only a very partial success, while France had taken revenge on Britain only at the cost of completing the ruin of her shaky finances and paving the way for the collapse of the old régime which began in 1787.

The two or three generations before the French Revolution were an age of warfare and aggression. It was generally accepted throughout the century that relations between the states of Europe were dominated by greed, fear, and envy. It was widely agreed that the moral laws which governed the conduct of individuals were not binding on governments, so that David Hume, the most acute philosopher of the age, could argue that 'we must necessarily give a greater indulgence to a prince or minister who deceives another; than to a private gentleman who breaks his word of honour.' The plans for international organization and permanent peace put forward by the Abbé de Saint-Pierre early in the century, and in a different form by such thinkers as Jeremy Bentham and Immanuel Kant in its later years, had no practical importance. The hostility of the Physiocrats (see p. 84) and of many other thinkers of the Enlightenment to such traditional aspects of international relations as the balance of power and secret diplomacy (a hostility which was to be echoed by many radicals during the nineteenth and twentieth centuries) had no more effect.

International relations during this period were therefore dominated by territorial changes (the destruction of the Spanish and Swedish empires in Europe, the spoliation of Poland, the conquest of Silesia) carried out by force. The most important result of these changes was the rise of two new great powers, Brandenburg-Prussia and above all Russia. For Poland their emergence meant eventual extinction, for Sweden and the Ottoman Empire the threat of domination by a great and expanding neighbour. For the Habsburg Empire, itself in many ways one of the growing powers of the period, it meant the end of unquestioned leadership in Germany and the beginnings of competition with Russia in the Balkans. From 1740 onwards the politics of central Europe took on a new shape, and Italian issues, so important during the first half of the century, sank rapidly into the background. From the 1760s onwards the problems of eastern and south-eastern Europe assumed a hitherto unknown importance. The fact that by the middle of the century a high proportion of the military resources of the continent was in the hands of states (Austria, Russia, and Prussia) which were all politically and economically backward was to have profound repercussions on the whole later history of Europe. France, in spite of her great resources, her continuing prestige, and the acquisition of Lorraine and Corsica, had been barely able to maintain her relative status among the powers. Spain was becoming merely the greatest of the secondary states. The colonial and economic achievements of Britain had not made her a true military power or given her any real interest in the affairs of Europe east of the Elbe or even perhaps of the Rhine. All this meant that the centre of gravity in European politics had moved perceptibly to the east.

In America and Asia, where the peasant armies of eastern and central Europe counted for nothing, the position was entirely different. Spain, formerly so much the greatest of all colonial powers, was now on the defensive. France, fatally handicapped by her European land frontiers and the traditional ambitions associated with them, had been decisively outdistanced by Britain. Aided by supreme naval power, by a highly developed economy, and by the ability to export population on a large scale, the latter, in spite of the catastrophe in America, was now well on the way to the position she was to hold for most of the first half of the nineteenth century—that of the only great imperial power and the only real industrial power in the world.

# 3
# Society and Economic Life

THE STRUCTURE OF European society, and of Europe's economy, remained remarkably stable during almost the whole of the eighteenth century. In both, change was slow, geographically uneven, and opposed by powerful traditions and vested interests. In both, nevertheless, more particularly in economic life, the forces of change were becoming more effective as the century drew to a close.

All over Europe society was still highly traditional. Almost everywhere it was taken for granted that deep social distinctions were inevitable. Only a few hardy spirits doubted that hereditary ruling groups and those subject to them had each their essential part to play in the workings of society and that the only legitimate objective of social change was to enable them to play it more effectively. Only a small educated minority fully understood that societies are the work of man and not of God. Only among this minority was there any belief that radical social change was possible. To the majority everywhere the idea that society could be remodelled deliberately on a more equal and rational basis was almost inconceivable and, when it was presented to them, repugnant. It seems likely that the widespread suspicion of Freemasonry was partly inspired by the tendency of many masonic lodges to recruit their members from a variety of social strata, and many governments actively discouraged marriages between members of different classes. The Spanish government, for example, did so in legislation of 1778. Occasionally, at least in the early decades of the century, a ruling class would be distinguished in the most obvious of all ways—by a special dress or some other sign of rank which it alone had the right to wear, or was even compelled to wear; thus in 1710 the Council of Ten in Venice threatened (ineffectively) to fine and imprison any noble who appeared in public without wearing his *vesta patrizia*. Even in England, in 1732 the King's Advocate exhibited a complaint in the High Court of Chivalry (which ceased to function five years later) against the widow of a merchant for using at her husband's funeral 'ensigns of honour not belonging to his condition'.

Traditional rights and the traditional social structure were normally quite strong enough to withstand very drastic political changes. It was universally agreed that mere military conquest of an area conveyed no right to tamper with the organization of society there. Thus when Louis XIV conquered Franche-Comté in 1674 he almost at once granted a capitulation to the *Parlement* of Dôle, the supreme legal institution of the province, by which he promised that 'everything shall remain in Franche-Comté as it is at present with regard to privileges, franchises, and immunities', and swore to protect all existing rights there. In the same way, when Strasbourg was annexed to France in 1681, it was allowed to retain its traditional constitution, a high degree of fiscal independence, and other important privileges; while Peter the Great of Russia, when he conquered the Swedish Baltic provinces, promised, notably by a proclamation of October 1710 addressed to the nobility and burghers of Livonia, to respect all existing rights and privileges there.

This traditional and highly conservative society was extremely complex. It varied enormously in different parts of the continent, so that the social structure of Russia or Poland had very little in common with that of England or the Dutch provinces. Even within the same state variations were enormous: for example in Spain Andalusia or La Mancha differed greatly from the Basque provinces of the northern coastline, and in Great Britain, until late in the century, the Highlands of Scotland seemed socially, as in many other ways, a foreign land to Lowland Scots as well as to Englishmen. Superimposed on these geographical differences and in many ways more import-

ant, was the fact that everywhere society was divided into small
and closely-knit groups—parishes, guilds, village communities,
municipalities. These had often a very high degree of autonomy
within their own spheres of activity and could affect the life of
the ordinary man far more directly and immediately than remote
and sometimes rather powerless central governments. The idea
that all citizens of a state should be equal in the eyes of the law,
that they should enjoy the same rights and be subject to the same
obligations, was still a strange and often unwelcome one over
most of Europe. Membership of a guild or a village community
conferred both privileges and duties unshared by non-members;
and this fact was accepted by governments, though with slowly
increasing reluctance as the century progressed. Even in 1791
the great Prussian law-code, the most ambitious and successful
of the period, recognized that 'civil society consists of many
small societies and estates, connected to each other by nature or
law, or by both together'. In Russia, backward, thinly-populated,
and with a highly-centralized and autocratic government, these
socio-economic groups were of little importance. In England,
which had for centuries enjoyed legal and administrative unity
and effective central government, they were also less important
than in many other parts of the continent. But over most of
Europe they formed, in differing degrees, the basis of society.

The task of describing this endlessly varied and complicated
social picture is made much more difficult by the almost total
lack of any precise terminology. In every part of Europe the
portmanteau terms—'nobility', 'peasantry', 'bourgeoisie', or
'middle classes'—which the historian is forced to use for lack
of any others, covered a number, often a large number, of
different social groups, sometimes with radically differing out-
looks and aspirations. A peasant in Normandy was no more the
same as one in Livonia than a member of the British House of
Lords resembled one of the poor and uneducated squires who
made up the vast majority of the Polish 'nobility'. A tradesman
in the capital of some minor German state, perhaps totally
dependent on the court and its hangers-on for custom, or the
owner of a workshop in some French provincial town, was a
different social being from one of the great merchant princes of

London or bankers of Amsterdam, though all can be described, with equal lack of meaning, as members of the 'middle class'.

Yet it is possible to make some valid generalizations about eighteenth-century society. In the first place, it scarcely needs to be said, it was a society dominated by men. It is true that in educated circles, particularly in France, there was a tendency for the status of women to improve, especially from the middle of the century onward: the increasing emphasis during the same period on more natural and spontaneous methods of bringing up children probably strengthened this tendency. But even the most radical contemporary writers on social and intellectual problems seldom spoke of women as in any way the equals of men; except among a few very advanced thinkers this idea was almost unknown.

Over much the greater part of Europe also, society was agrarian. Towns and all they stood for were relatively unimportant. Material well-being, to an extent hard to grasp today, depended on the state of the harvest and was thus at the mercy of natural forces. This overwhelming economic importance of agriculture except in a few favoured and advanced areas was the most important explanation of the conservatism of European society.

The nobility, in the sense of a legally privileged ruling class, was so heterogeneous as to defy brief description. Over most of Europe there was a fundamental distinction between the greater nobles, often enormously wealthy, and the lesser ones, who were far more numerous and often distinguishable from peasants only by their legally privileged status. In Spain, for example, the census of 1787 revealed the existence of 119 grandees (themselves divided, in theory, into three different grades and intermarrying only with other grandee families), 535 *titulos* (titled persons), and half a million *hidalgos*, most of whom were relatively poor and many of whom were very poverty-stricken indeed. In Poland society and political life were dominated by a small number of enormously rich and powerful families: in 1770 Stanislaus Lubomirski, Palatin of Braclaw, owned 31 towns and 776 villages, and two decades later Felix Potocki was alleged to possess 130,000 serfs and to have an income of three million florins. Yet side by side with these very wealthy nobles existed scores of thousands of poor and uneducated squires (*szlachta*) who, though legally privileged, were in no real sense members of the same class. In Hungary the contrast between the great families such as the Esterhazys and Palffys and the poor, backward, and bitterly conservative squirearchy was equally abrupt; it was accentuated by the fact that the former had usually remained Catholic during the Reformation or had been reconverted to Catholicism during the seventeenth century, while the latter largely remained Calvinist. Even in France, where the 'nobility' made up a smaller proportion of the population than in Poland, Spain, or Hungary, there was a great gulf, and much resentment and ill-feeling, between the greater families who had access to the court and increasingly monopolized the major offices in church and state and the poor country nobility (*hobereaux*) who did not enjoy these advantages. In Brittany, the poorest of French provinces, nobles can be found during the middle decades of the century earning a living as a steward, a gamekeeper, a muleteer, and even a wig-maker. In Russia and most of Germany the contrast between the greater and lesser nobles was perhaps rather less striking, during much of the century at least, than in some other parts of Europe; but even there it was marked. Of all the major states only Great Britain and Sweden possessed nobilities which were relatively small, well-defined, and homogeneous groups. Increasingly, as the century progressed, the greater nobles in many parts of Europe attempted to maintain their estates intact and to prevent their dispersal among a multitude of heirs. In Britain primogeniture, entails, and the device of the 'strict settlement' achieved this with almost complete success. The *mayorazgo* in Spain, the *Fideikommiss* in the German states, were designed to attain the same end and thus tended to perpetuate in these areas the distinction between greater and lesser nobles.

Everywhere the nobility was, above all, a class of landowners. But the extent to which it predominated in landownership, and the manner in which it exploited its lands and rights over land, differed widely in different areas. In some parts of Europe—Naples, Sicily, southern Spain, Lithuania and eastern Poland, much of eastern Germany—the structure of agrarian life was dominated by the existence of large, sometimes enormous, estates. Elsewhere, for example over much of France and western Germany, very large unified estates were much rarer and there was a considerable element of relatively well-to-do peasantry, farmers, and smallholders. In yet other parts of the continent, notably in England, the Lowlands of Scotland, and Sweden, great landowners tended increasingly to lease land to tenant farmers, usually in fairly large parcels and for fairly long periods. Almost everywhere in eastern and much of central Europe landowning was the prerogative of the nobility. In Russia and Brandenburg-Prussia, where this class had been transformed into one of hereditary state-servants by powerful and energetic rulers (the Great Elector and Frederick William I in Prussia, Peter I in Russia), the governments were compelled to take active measures to preserve the right to landownership of these indispensible subordinates. In Russia the *dvoryanstvo*—this class of landowners, bureaucrats, and officers—succeeded in 1746–7 in forcing the Empress Elizabeth to grant them the exclusive right to the ownership of land with peasant serfs. In Prussia the corresponding *junker* class was protected by repeated orders of Frederick II that no land owned by nobles should be sold to non-nobles without his express consent; while in 1775 middle-class owners of former noble land were forbidden to leave it by will to middle-class heirs. In the Habsburg dominions, in almost all eastern and much of central Germany, and in large areas of Italy and Spain it was rare to find much land not owned by the nobility or the Catholic church. On the other hand in England and France considerable amounts were being acquired by merchants, tradesmen, professional men (above all lawyers), and even manufacturers, while in Piedmont in northern Italy as early as the beginning of the century the nobility and clergy together held only about 25 to 30 per cent. of the land, a very low figure. In these areas the gulf between noble and bourgeois, though still very real, could be bridged by money; the social rigidities of the impoverished east were less noticeable.

Everywhere the ownership of land conferred, in varying degrees, social and political power. Almost everywhere governments had to rely upon landowners as their agents in the administration and control of the countryside. Almost everywhere the greater landowners were able to exact from governments important privileges, above all fiscal ones, as the price of their cooperation. These factors were again most clearly visible in eastern and east-central Europe. The Hungarian nobility, one of the proudest and most selfish of all, succeeded in 1731 in asserting its right to pay no taxes whatever. Until 1768 its Polish counterpart enjoyed the power of life and death over its peasant serfs. In the same way in Russia, from the death of Peter I onwards, his weaker successors were driven into a series of concessions to the landowners which culminated in 1762 in the formal abolition of their legal obligation to serve the state in the bureaucracy or the armed forces (though in fact, for various reasons, the great majority of them continued to serve in these ways for long after this date). But in the most advanced states of western Europe the position was not radically different. In France the nobility, still essentially a landowning class, enjoyed very important fiscal privileges, notably in respect of the *taille*, the major tax on real estate. In Spain, until late in the century, there was a tendency for the great nobles to regard important administrative positions as beneath their dignity and to prefer to hold merely decorative court appointments. But even there it was not until 1795 that the last legal distinction between nobles and commoners in respect of taxation was abolished. In England, where the nobility in the strict sense was a uniquely small and well-defined body enjoying no legal privileges of much practical importance, local government in the countryside was completely dominated by the justices of the peace recruited from the more substantial landowners and the clergy (the two categories often overlapped).

Above all it was from this privileged landowning class, often from its poorer members in particular, that European armies recruited their officers. There are few examples in the eighteenth century of anyone rising to really high military rank merely by merit and without any advantages of birth. In eastern Europe it could be plausibly argued that landowners alone possessed the ability to command and the rudimentary education needed by an officer. It was also asserted, notably by Frederick II, that a nobleman possessed ideas of duty, self-sacrifice, and personal honour which a commoner could not be expected to have. Everywhere, moreover, young and poor noblemen found in military service an outlet, often the only one available, for their energies and talents, and an indispensable source of income. This explains the bitterness with which they regarded, most notably in France in the middle and later decades of the century, any introduction of non-nobles into the officer-corps.

Besides their great economic and administrative powers the nobility enjoyed, to varying extents, personal privileges and exemptions in almost all parts of Europe. They were usually exempt from torture and from certain punishments which were regarded as degrading (for example, death by hanging as opposed to the more dignified method of decapitation). They were often exempt from imprisonment for debt and (for example in Spain and in the last years of this period in Russia) from having troops billeted in their houses. At universities nobles were often given privileged treatment and allowed to take degrees more quickly and easily than commoners. In the later decades of the century, at least in western Europe, it was these obtrusive and irritating personal privileges as much as the real power of the traditional ruling class which stimulated middle-class resentment.

The men who worked the land were even less socially homogeneous than those who owned it. They were divided in the first place by the distinction, of great legal importance though often of less economic significance, between serfs and free men. Serfdom was essentially a characteristic of eastern and parts of central Europe. In the British Isles, the Netherlands, Spain, and Italy it did not exist. In France serfs (*mainmortables*) were to be found only in a few areas in the east of the country, and in west and south-west Germany they were relatively rare. In much of Brandenburg-Prussia, on the other hand, the rural population was composed of serfs; and the power of the landlords, backed by the state which they served as officials, magistrates, and army officers, was very extensive. Over much of the

Habsburg territories serfdom was still a dominant social institution. In Poland the position of the serfs was so bad that in 1698 an observer compared it to that of Negro slaves in the West Indies; and in Russia, where Peter I had done so much to extend serfdom, it became increasingly oppressive and widespread throughout the century. In 1760 Russian landowners were given the power to exile to Siberia lazy or rebellious serfs, and two years later were allowed to transfer serfs from one of their estates to another. Moreover the labour-services which the Russian serf had to perform for his lord were constantly tending to grow in the second half of the century. No social group in Europe saw its position deteriorate more sharply than did the Russian peasantry during this period.

This contrast between the eastern and western parts of the continent was intensified by the fact that in western and much of central Europe, where serfdom existed, it was increasingly frowned upon by governments and regarded as a shameful heritage of the past. In Lorraine, in Savoy, and most notably in the German state of Baden, the century saw its legal abolition. In the Habsburg Empire Joseph II, the greatest and most tragic reforming monarch of the age (see pp. 95–7) granted the serfs in his dominions personal freedom in 1781, though he did not abolish labour-service. In Russia on the other hand serfdom, as has been seen, was still very much a growing institution, and in Prussia Frederick II did no more than tinker with the problem of its abolition: even on the royal estates it was swept away only in 1799–1805. Dead or moribund in the west, it was still one of the dominant forces in east European society.

But all these generalizations can be endlessly qualified. Serfdom is not a precise term, and the reality for which it stood differed widely between one area and another. The serfs who still remained in France or western Germany, for example, were normally much better off than those of Pomerania or East Prussia. Areas of agrarian freedom existed side by side with others of intensive serfdom: so that in north Russia, where the population was thinly scattered and the land infertile, serfdom hardly existed at a time when in the central areas around Moscow its weight was often crushing. Almost everywhere peasants on crown lands tended to be considerably better off than those on the estates of private landowners.

Serfdom in eastern Europe tended to reduce those subject to it to a common level of powerlessness and to iron out the distinctions which had hitherto existed between different groups in peasant society. Over much of western Europe the free agrarian population presented a picture of greater variety and complexity. In France, for example, there were, especially in the richer areas, a considerable number of large tenant farmers who sometimes formed a closed social group, intermarrying and succeeding each other from father to son on the land they rented from some noble. Side by side with these substantial farms were many medium-sized peasant holdings whose owners (*laboureurs*) possessed or rented enough land to maintain themselves and their families and who usually owned their own implements and livestock. Finally, at the bottom of the rural hierarchy, were the farm-servants and hired labourers (*manoeuvriers*) who could never rise above the level of subsistence and who all too often fell below it. And these very broad categories can be subdivided and qualified almost endlessly to take account of regional variations in the productivity of the soil, the law of landownership, the density of the population, and other factors. (In particular the system of *métayage* or share-cropping, which was common in much of southern and western France, introduces considerable complications.) The position was almost equally complex in other and less studied parts of Europe. Thus in Spain there was an obvious contrast between the peasant who worked as a day-labourer on a *latifundio* in Andalusia and the Basque farmer cultivating his own patch of land. There was at least as great a difference between the substantial tenant farmer in a reasonably fertile part of England and the average inhabitant of the Highlands of Scotland, where the system of landholding remained archaic and largely tribal until the second half of the century.

It is clear that in many areas during the eighteenth century the rural proletariat, the segment of agrarian society which had very little or no land, was growing in numbers and finding it increasingly difficult to live. This was certainly the case in

France, where the rise in population (from 18 million to 26 million in 1715-89) led to marked rural overpopulation and unemployment, with a resulting rise in vagrancy, in the number of beggars, and in social tensions in the countryside. Moreover there was a tendency during the third quarter of the century for food prices to rise, making it more and more difficult for the man with no source of livelihood but his own labour to keep himself and his family. In Italy, as in France, the position of day-labourers was clearly deteriorating, especially after about 1760: in the later decades of the century they could not earn enough to keep themselves and their families properly fed. On the other hand high food prices, enclosures of common land, and sales of land by impoverished nobles, all tended in many areas to strengthen the position of the better-off peasantry. It was this group which in France, and to a lesser extent elsewhere in western Europe, benefited most from the revolutionary changes at the end of the century.

It is in the towns that social change is most noticeable in the eighteenth century. A few great cities were now growing very rapidly, and by the later decades of this period Europe boasted a number of urban centres of hitherto unprecedented size. By the 1780s London, the biggest of all, had about 850,000 inhabitants, Paris 650,000, and Amsterdam and Vienna about 200,000 each. Such cities, by their very size and by the speed with which some of them were growing, were difficult to fit into the traditional and largely static pattern which dominated the rest of European society. The distrust of the country-dweller for the city which was so notable a characteristic of much of eighteenth-century Europe was perhaps increased by their growth; but with all their defects London and Paris, or even Liverpool, Marseilles, or Hamburg, were not parochial in the way that villages and small country towns all over Europe very notably were. Moreover the large town was a centre of intellectual activity. It might well be the seat of a university or a learned society (though neither of these was in this period an infallible sign of a vigorous intellectual life—see pp. 123-4); and in the last decades of the century it was increasingly likely, in Britain, Germany, and to a lesser extent France, to have a newspaper of its own (see p. 125). In such an environment unthinking sub-mission to the existing structure of society was much less likely than in the countryside.

Above all it was in the towns that there developed the com-mercial, industrial, and professional middle class; and the growth of this group, or rather series of groups, was the most important social development in western Europe during this period. The highest reaches of urban society were even at the end of the century almost entirely the product of trade and finance, not of industry or the professions. The urban patriciate of Amsterdam, its fortunes built on trade and banking, is perhaps the supreme illustration of the predominance of com-mercial and financial interests in the great European cities. It can be paralleled in London, where again banking and merchant interests were dominant; or to a lesser extent in Paris, where tax-farming and government loans and contracts played a large part in the rise of a small but very wealthy and powerful *grande bourgeoisie*; or in Hamburg, now developing brilliantly as a sea-port and a centre of finance and insurance. No industrialist of the period could hope to acquire the social standing or the political influence of a great London merchant such as Sir Joshua Vanneck, a great Paris financier such as Samuel Bernard, or a great Dutch banking dynasty such as the Hopes'. James Watt, who has certainly as good a claim as anyone to be con-sidered the architect of the Industrial Revolution, could write in 1787 that 'our landed gentlemen reckon us poor mechanics no better than slaves who cultivate their vineyards'. Moreover the professions, nowadays so important a component of the middle class, were still only in process of development. Physicians were already of some social standing and lawyers were steadily becom-ing more socially respectable, at least in Britain, where a good many existing firms of solicitors can trace their origins to attorneys practising in the second half of the eighteenth cen-tury. But many of the modern professions simply did not yet exist, and those that did were often still loosely organized and finding it difficult to maintain rigid professional standards.

Besides this small but wealthy upper middle class of mer-chants, bankers, and financiers, the cities of western Europe included in their population a growing lower middle class element composed of tradesmen, master craftsmen, and small merchants. This in its turn was often highly subdivided; for in many cities the craft guilds were arranged in a recognized hierarchy with such groups as goldsmiths at the top and lesser ones beneath them. Relations between the wealthy upper middle class and those more or less immediately beneath it were often very strained and sometimes actively hostile. The poorer members of the middle class often bitterly resented the dominant position normally held by the wealthy in city government. In many cities, those of Germany and Switzerland in particular, control had for generations been in the hands of merchant oligarchies whose members intermarried and who jealously excluded all other inhabitants from power . Often this oligarchical control was enshrined in the city constitution. This was the case for example in Berne, where about 250 families were classified as capable of holding public office (*regimentsfähig*) and about seventy of these in fact controlled the city. The position was similar in Geneva, where a body known as the Two Hundred monopolized office in the ruling Small Council. Indeed these urban privileged groups were often far more exclusive and difficult for an outsider to enter than the nobilities of most of the great European states.

Oligarchical control of this kind was becoming more and more unpopular in the cities of the more advanced parts of western Europe during the later decades of the century. In Geneva, the Burghers, the second of the three classes into which the population was divided, secured some political power in 1768, after a genuine though limited revolution in the city, only to see the old oligarchical constitution restored with French help in 1782. In the same way, though with less overt violence, there was conflict at Worms between the artisan population and the oligarchy which controlled the ruling Council of Thirteen; while in Aix-la-Chapelle a struggle between the 'new' and 'old' parties, who had elected different burgomasters, was still going on when the armies of the French Revolution entered the city in 1792. In a somewhat similar way the radicalism to be seen in London in the 1760s and 1770s, with its demands for shorter parliaments, a widening of the parliamentary suffrage, and a reduction of aristocratic and royal power, drew a good deal of its strength from the envy felt by tradesmen and craftsmen for the great merchants and bankers whose close connexions with the government they distrusted and disliked. The same kind of social conflict can be seen once more in the alarm aroused among the urban patriciate of Amsterdam and the other great Dutch towns by the radicalism of the pro-French Patriot party in 1786–7 and in their turning to their traditional opponents, the House of Orange, for protection.

The growth and vitality of the great cities thus expressed itself partly in the form of intensified social antagonisms which largely drain of meaning the overworked term 'middle classes'. But it must be remembered that really dangerous tensions of this kind were confined to a relatively small number of towns even in western Europe. Geneva might be racked by conflict; but in other Swiss and German cities, even some which were flourishing economically—Basle, Zürich, Augsburg, Frank-furt-on-Main, Hamburg—the traditional ruling groups were able to keep control without much difficulty until they were swept away, in most cases, by the armies of revolutionary France. More important, there were many great urban centres in western Europe which did not provide the environment in which a powerful commercial and financial bourgeoisie could flourish. In Italy towns such as Florence, Venice, or Rome, still in terms of population among the most important in Europe, were political capitals rather than trading or financial centres. In them the court with its servants and officials played a great part in economic life, as it did in German princely capitals such as Mannheim, Karlsruhe, or even Berlin. In all these the con-spicuous expenditure of rulers, nobles, officials, and sometimes tourists was essential to prosperity; cities such as these were centres of consumption and display rather than of production or trade. Even in Naples, the largest of Italian towns and an important port, a large part of the population existed merely as the hangers-on and dependants of a handful of nobles. 'The profession of 15,000 people at Naples,' complained a French traveller in 1786, 'is to run ahead of a carriage, and of 15,000 others to run behind.' Towns of this kind were fundamentally different from London, Amsterdam, Bordeaux, Marseilles, Bristol, Liverpool, or Hamburg. For all their size they had nothing to offer the future. In Spain, where the intellectual and social climate was even less favourable to large-scale trade and finance than in many parts of Italy, Barcelona and Bilbao were the only cities in which modern urban attitudes and values were dominant. The once-important towns of Castile—Avila, Saragossa, Toledo, Valladolid—were living in the past even more completely than Venice or Rome.

Above all, the urban power and bourgeois self-confidence to be seen in some parts of western Europe were completely lacking in the eastern half of the continent. In Poland, Brandenburg-Prussia, the Habsburg Empire, and Russia towns were almost all small. In 1772 there were only five towns in Poland with over 20,000 inhabitants; and though by the end of the century the population of Warsaw had grown rapidly to about 100,000 the city never played in Polish history the role of London or Amsterdam in England or the Dutch Republic. In Hungary the position was very similar: in 1777 there were also five towns with populations greater than 20,000; the largest, Debrecen, numbered only 30,000 inhabitants. Ten years later a census returned only five thousand as professional men or civil servants out of a total Hungarian population of six-and-a-half million. Moreover in Poland and Hungary the towns that existed were often hardly Polish or Hungarian at all. Much of their population was composed of Jews, sometimes of Greeks or Armenians, above all of Germans. Danzig, theoretically a part of Poland, was in fact a completely German city; and until the 1880s the town council of Budapest transacted its business in German. In St. Petersburg and the ports of the Baltic provinces, again, large-scale trade was overwhelmingly in the hands of foreigners, notably Englishmen. The few eastern and central European cities which were not small, or in some way foreign to the areas in which they were situated, were usually, like Berlin and Vienna, political capitals and thus largely dependent for their prosperity on courts and governments. Under these circumstances the dynamism, the economic progress and social flux, which urban growth was bringing to some parts of western Europe, was greatly weakened. East of the Rhine substantial change of any kind had to be brought about from above, as the work of rulers and governments. It could not be produced from below.

Except in a few areas, therefore, European society in the eighteenth century was hostile to change. Almost everywhere it was still dominated by hereditary privilege, by landowners, nobilities, and urban oligarchies. In many states in the second half of the century there was even a tendency for the dominance of these groups to become more marked and obtrusive. In France, where this phenomenon has been most intensively studied, it became in the last decades of the old régime increasingly difficult for a bourgeois to achieve nobility, whether by the purchase of a government office which conferred this status or by other methods. Under Louis XVI not a single bishop was of non-noble origin. Nor were any of the *intendants*, the great officials who, each in his own area (*généralité*), controlled the administration and much of the life of provincial France. In 1781 the access of bourgeois to army commissions was drastically reduced. Moreover even within the nobility there was a tendency for the older families to increase their predominance. Not only were virtually all the highest offices of state in France held by nobles during the three generations before the revolution, but over half of them were occupied by members of families which had been noble for more than two centuries and over a quarter by members of those noble for more than three. While the French nobility was alienating the middle classes by this reassertion of its supremacy and of the claims of ancestry it was simultaneously antagonizing the peasantry. This it did by an increasingly rigid assertion of its feudal rights—rights of jurisdiction; its right in some areas to force the peasant to use his lord's mill, oven, wine-press, etc. and to pay for their use; its right to a rent in kind (*champart*) and to payments (*lods et ventes*) when peasant land changed hands. More and more these rights were being commercialized, used simply as sources of income and exploited to the full for this purpose. More and more the French nobility were using efficient accounting procedures in the running of their estates, having the boundaries of their lands accurately mapped, specifying with unheard-of precision the dues owed them by the peasants, and sometimes demanding payment of those which had long been allowed to lapse. It was becoming increasingly common, at least in some areas, for landlords to make loans in cash or kind to their tenants and to seize the tenants' land in default of payment. Widespread enclosure of common land was tending to enlarge noble estates over much of France. The conventional phrase 'feudal reaction' which is often used to describe all these developments is rather misleading. What was happening was not a reassertion of true feudal ideas or attitudes but rather the conscious use of surviving relics of feudalism in France for purely commercial purposes.

Nowhere else in Europe did this process go so far as in France, because nowhere else was a largely feudal system of land law and landownership combined with a social structure so increasingly dominated by commercial forces. Everywhere, however, the landed ruling class was active in the defence of its position. In Russia some of the *dvoryanstvo*, under the influence of the Imperial Free Economic Society founded in 1765, attempted, with varying success, to run their estates on more modern and efficient lines; but few of them showed real willingness to face the implications of serfdom for their own future and that of the country. Moreover Catherine II in 1785, in her Charter to the Nobility, provided for the drawing-up of genealogical registers of the *dvoryanstvo* in each province—an important step towards making it a better-defined and more exclusive group. In the western territories of Brandenburg-Prussia, the Estates of Minden-Ravensberg, dominated by the nobility, in 1791 refused to recognize the legitimacy of marriages between nobles and commoners, or to pay the compensation imposed by the new code of laws promulgated in that year upon nobles who had children by their serf-girls. In Piedmont the share-cropping system under which much land was cultivated became steadily more favourable to the noble landowner throughout the century; as population and the demand for land grew so did his proportion of the crop. Even in England it

became more difficult after about 1750 to move from the merchant class into the landowning one, and a recent historian has
asserted that 'the social distance between landed and commercial classes had perhaps never been greater in England than
in the days of Jane Austen and on the eve of the First Reform
Bill'. Over much of Europe in the later eighteenth century class
distinctions were becoming sharper and more resented. The
revolution which this resentment helped to produce in France
could thus rely on widespread if often covert sympathy in
many other states.

The growth in western Europe of towns, of trade, and of
middle-class discontent with the existing social system were all
the results of economic development. But progress in this
sphere was slow until the last decades of the century and very
uneven in its effect upon different parts of the continent and
different types of economic activity.

In one respect economic life was clearly advancing: Europe's
population was growing rapidly. In 1700 the continent had a
population of perhaps 118 million; by 1750 this had increased
to about 140 million and by 1800 to 187 million. The accelerated growth after the middle of the century which these figures
reveal was shared by almost every part of Europe: for example
the population of England and Wales in the first half of the
century increased at an annual rate of only 5,000 to 8,000; from
the 1760s onwards the growth was of the order of 60,000 a
year. At the beginning of the century England and Wales had
5 million inhabitants; at its end, in spite of appreciable emigration, they had 9 million. This was a rate of increase which few
other states could match. But the population of France rose
from 18 million in 1715 to 26 million at the time of the Revolution, that of Italy from perhaps 11 million to more than 16
million in 1700–70, and that of Spain from perhaps 8 million to
11 million during the century.

This unprecedented growth in the number of Europeans was
caused almost entirely by an improvement in the continent's
food-supply. Except in a few states, notably Sweden, population
statistics for the period are patchy and unreliable. But so far as

they go they indicate a strong tendency, normal in all pre-modern societies, for the birth-rate to rise and the death-rate to fall when harvests were good and food plentiful. Conversely the birth-rate fell sharply and the death-rate rose in periods of bad harvest and high food prices. Compared to the effects of the food-supply those of medical advances (the most notable was the introduction of vaccination against smallpox) were of very minor importance even in the parts of Europe where they were widely applied. And though every country suffered at times during the eighteenth century from more or less acute shortages of food, absolute famine on a large scale was becoming increasingly rare and in some parts of Europe unknown. It was still by no means a thing of the past: in Sicily and Naples in 1763-4, in Saxony and Bohemia in 1770, there was genuine and widespread starvation. Wretchedly bad roads and the resulting difficulty in moving bulky commodities such as grain, which was almost the only food of tens of millions of people, meant that it was still possible for a province to starve while another part of the same state enjoyed relative plenty. But in France there was no real famine, as distinct from mere shortage, later than the terrible winter of 1709; and in Britain really acute crises of this kind were now merely a memory. It was this more abundant and reliable food-supply which, by encouraging early marriage and a high birth-rate and by increasing resistance to disease, particularly to epidemics, produced such remarkable demographic growth.

The results of this rise in population are hard to measure with any certainty, but some of their main outlines are unmistakable. It meant that the rise in Europe's output of food had to be sustained. This was achieved by more efficient methods of cultivation, as in much of Britain and the Netherlands and a few areas of France; or by a large extension of the area under cultivation, as in Russia and to some extent Poland and Prussia; or by the extended cultivation of new crops, above all potatoes and maize, which slowly reduced the continent's dangerous dependence on one or two staple cereals. In many parts of Europe—much of France, Spain, and Italy, for example—population growth led, as has already been pointed out, to increased peasant demand for land, to a strengthening of the position of landlords as against their tenants, and to increased social tensions in the countryside. It provided a growing market for the products of the relatively sophisticated machine-based industries which were struggling into existence in a few areas, and also the labour-force needed to man them. In the Highlands of Scotland and parts of Switzerland and west Germany it stimulated extensive emigration to the new lands of America or, more rarely, of Russia.

Population growth was the one truly revolutionary process at work in the economic life of Europe during most of the eighteenth century. By 1780 another and more spectacular one was visible. This was the rise in a few favoured parts of western Europe, above all in Britain, of a new type of industrial organization dependent on the labour of strictly controlled and disciplined workers brought together in large factories and using expensive machinery. During the eighteenth century this system was confined in the main to the textile industries; later it was to spread very much more widely. The evolution of the new system was rapid considering the magnitude of the changes it involved. The Industrial Revolution was truly revolutionary. It involved a leap from one level of economic organization, one system of production, to another, unmistakably higher, one. It was the most sudden and important break with the past that humanity has ever made.

This leap was made possible partly by a series of important inventions and technological changes in British industry, most of which are well known. In the textile industries, above all in the cotton industry, production was revolutionized by the invention of the 'flying shuttle' in the early 1730s, the 'spinning-jenny' in 1768, the power spinning-frame in 1769, the mule in 1779, and cotton-printing machinery in 1783. In the early 1770s Richard Arkwright built at Cromford, near Derby, a large cotton mill which has been described as 'perhaps the first true factory'. By the end of the century the metal-producing and metal-working industries were being changed equally fundamentally by the increasing use, from about 1720 onwards, of coke as a fuel for iron-smelting, by the introduction of the puddling process in the production of iron (1784), by the use of the crucible method of steel-making, and by the accelerated development of machine tools. From the middle 1770s onwards the power needed to drive new machinery of all kinds was beginning to be provided by the most far-reaching innovation of all, the new and much more efficient type of steam-engine developed by James Watt. (The first Watt engines had an overall thermal efficiency of about 2.7 per cent.—almost twice that of even the improved version of the earlier Newcomen engines.)

But ingenious technical devices were in themselves nothing new. Since the later Middle Ages Italy and the mining areas of Germany in particular had produced them in large numbers; yet neither country gave rise to an industrial revolution. Nor is it even quite certain that more mechanical and technical innovations were made in Britain in the eighteenth than in the seventeenth century. What is certain is that they were more economically valuable than those of any earlier period and that they were more rapidly and generally applied. The really interesting and difficult question is why it was in Britain alone, and not before the later eighteenth century, that the leap to a new type of industry was made. The growing availability in Britain by the middle of the century of capital derived from growing agricultural productivity and to a lesser extent from growing trade, domestic as well as with Europe and the colonies, certainly provides part of the explanation. Some recent work on the problem has tended to stress, perhaps to overstress, the importance in this connexion of the generally low rates of interest at which money could be borrowed in Britain during the second half of the century. But it would certainly be an oversimplification to say that relatively plentiful capital caused the Industrial Revolution. Saving and investment were at least as much a result as a cause of economic growth, and the amount of capital needed to finance the early stages of industrialization was not exceptionally large. In Britain a high degree of physical security coupled with a relatively fair and efficient fiscal system provided a background which favoured economic enterprise. Such an environment helped to produce and spread a more aggressive and adventurous attitude to economic life, one which welcomed or at least accepted change and stressed more than in the past the maximum exploitation of resources and opportunities. The contribution of these non-economic factors to industrial development is impossible to measure exactly, but it must have been considerable. Population growth, above all, by increasing the domestic demand for industrial goods, had encouraging indirect effects: it is difficult to imagine changes in industry of this kind and magnitude within the framework of a falling population, and the Industrial Revolution developed against the background of a generally buoyant home market. (But once again we are faced by a cause-and-effect problem, for population increase was the result as much as the cause of economic growth, and there were many parts of eighteenth-century Europe whose populations grew sharply without any resulting transformation of their economic life.) Again the general improvement of communications in Britain, notably by the building of something like 3,000 miles of canals from the 1750s onwards, undoubtedly laid some of the foundations for industrial growth by providing a more unified domestic market. Finally, more immediate and short-run factors may have played some part; it has recently been argued that more difficult conditions in the British textile industries for several years after about 1762—relatively expensive credit and high prices for raw cotton—encouraged the rapid adoption of new cost-reducing machines. There are strong arguments in economic theory, moreover, for the thesis that once swift growth has begun in important sectors of an economy (in Britain, in cotton textiles and the metal industries), thus throwing it to some extent out of balance, this growth is certain to be transmitted before long to other aspects of economic life.

The importance of these economic changes in Britain can be easily illustrated. They led to an enormous expansion in the production of certain basic manufactured goods and materials, above all cotton textiles, iron, and coal. The number of blast-furnaces, for example, multiplied about five-fold in the generation 1760–90, and the number of cotton-spindles doubled in the two decades 1780–1800. This vast increase was achieved without any significant rise in the price of most industrial products, though wages and living standards generally were rising: a writer in 1808 calculated that during the previous seventy years the price of a ton of coal mined in Scotland had increased by only 2d. though the cost of the labour and materials used to produce it had doubled. Abundance and relative cheapness meant a vast increase in British exports of manufactured goods and hence in imports of raw materials (above all raw cotton) in the last years of the century. It has been calculated that in the period 1700–70 the average annual increase in Britain's overseas trade was 1·2 per cent; in the 1780s it was four times as much. By then the beginnings of British industrial dominance of the world were clearly visible. Again the concentration of the new machines in large factories and the need to keep them running constantly throughout the working day meant the gathering of unprecedented numbers of workers in single productive units and their subjection to strict industrial discipline. This in turn meant the beginnings of a new social group—the modern industrial working class.

Nevertheless neither the physical scale nor the geographical scope of these new industrial developments should be exaggerated. All the steam-engines produced during the later eighteenth century by the firm of Boulton and Watt had together a total output of only about 7,500 horsepower. A hundred years later single engines producing twice as much were not uncommon. To the end of the century and after, the availability of running water for use as a source of power did more than any other factor to decide the location of industry in Britain, and factories could still be severely hampered in their working by prolonged drought. In the summer of 1767, for example, the Carron iron-works at Falkirk, the most famous of the period, were at a standstill for three months for this reason. Large sectors of British industry were as yet hardly affected at all by the new machines or the factory system.

More important still, the new mode of production had merely begun to spread to a few parts of continental Europe by the end of the century. The first Watt steam-engine was installed in a German factory only in 1785. By 1790, when Britain possessed about two hundred factories for the spinning of cotton thread, there were only eight in France, all of them using British machinery. (These figures are open to some qualification, since 'factory' is not a precise term; but the contrast they point is undoubtedly a valid one.) In the later eighteenth century there were parts of continental Europe which were relatively highly industrialized. There were important metal-working industries in parts of the Austrian Netherlands and western Germany, large linen and woollen industries in Silesia and Bohemia, a considerable cotton-spinning industry developing in Catalonia. But almost everywhere except in Britain industrial organization and techniques remained essentially what they had been for decades, even generations.

Large industrial enterprises had existed in continental Europe throughout the century but, with a few exceptions such as the great Van Robais textile factory at Abbeville, which at the height of its success may have employed 3,000 people, they were not usually of a modern kind dependent on the labour of hired workers. More often their labour-force was in varying degrees unfree, composed of criminals, orphans, vagabonds, foundlings, and sometimes of soldiers or, in eastern Europe, of serfs. The very important iron and copper industries which developed in the southern Ural area of Russia from the early eighteenth century onwards, originally in response to the demands of the war with Sweden, depended heavily on the labour of serfs 'ascribed' to the foundries. On a smaller scale many Russian landowners attempted to develop on their estates industries using locally-produced raw materials and the labour of their serfs, and the same phenomenon was widespread in Poland, Prussia, and the Habsburg territories. There some of these noble-owned factories, such as that for the manufacture of woollen cloth set up by Count Waldstein on his lands in Bohemia in 1713, were of considerable importance. Indeed the advantage which landowners enjoyed over middle-class industrialists through their control of supplies of cheap labour was an important reason for the slowness with which a prosperous middle class developed over much of eastern and central Europe. Factories operated largely by unfree labour and using relatively primitive methods

were, whatever their size, different from those of a textile mag-
nate such as Arkwright or a great ironmaster such as John
Wilkinson in Britain. They reflected and perpetuated a less
sophisticated type of economic organization, one in which capital, skilled labour, and technical knowledge were scarcer.
Moreover where they existed, notably in the textile industries,
they were usually confined to the finishing processes, the
fulling, dyeing, and bleaching of the cloth. The typical method
of production in most European industries, again notably
in the textile industries, was the 'domestic system'.

Under this system, whose details varied considerably, the
spinner or weaver worked up in his own home raw or semi-
manufactured materials supplied to him, either directly or
through an intermediary, by the manufacturer, who organized
the whole process of production. Quite often the primitive
machines which he used were hired by him from the manufacturer. The goods he produced were then finished in a factory
owned by the manufacturer before being sent to market. Industrial organization of this kind was becoming increasingly widespread during the eighteenth century, largely because it allowed
the manufacturer to circumvent guild restrictions which attempted to prevent, in the interests of the master-craftsmen who
dominated the guilds, the growth in the towns of large-scale
industry. Its spread meant that many industries largely escaped
from the towns, especially in eastern and central Europe, and
took refuge in the countryside from which they drew their
labour-force. Thus in Bohemia during much of the century
about 200,000 domestic workers were employed in flax-spin-
ning, and in Britain in the 1750s one sail-maker in Warrington
claimed that he had formerly employed 5,000 such workers on
his own account.

The domestic system was thus one of the most important
elements in the economic life of Europe. It employed, at least
on a part-time basis, very large numbers of people, and underlay
a great part of the continent's industrial production. Moreover
by the degree of organization which it called for and the capital
investment it required, especially in stocks of raw materials, it
marked a great advance in sophistication as well as in scale over

the handicraft production which it had largely supplanted. Nevertheless it was not modern industry; it did not look forward to the nineteenth and even to the twentieth century as some branches of industry in Britain were beginning to do by the end of this period.

In trade and finance, as in industry, eighteenth-century Europe saw steady and sometimes rapid advance along lines already laid down rather than revolutionary change. The economic literature of the period deals largely with commercial questions; yet it was only in one or two west European countries that foreign trade played a vital part in economic life. Of these Britain and the Dutch Republic were the outstanding examples. Britain's trade grew more rapidly than that of any other state during the century: by 1800 the tonnage of the British merchant fleet was perhaps five or six times as big as it had been a hundred years earlier. But this growth was uneven both geographically and chronologically. Britain's trade with her colonies, above all with the American colonies and the West Indies, increased much more rapidly than her European trade; and, within Europe, the Baltic and Mediterranean countries tended to become more important as her trading partners and France and the German states relatively less so. Also the rate of increase of British trade was higher in the second half of the century than in the first, and accelerated sharply in its last decades. Throughout the period, however, Britain's seaborne commerce provided one of the bases of her political as of her economic strength. It was its growth, much more than her industrial development or her fiscal and financial innovations, which impressed contemporaries and aroused their envy.

The Dutch, the greatest commercial rivals of England in the later seventeenth and early eighteenth centuries, fared less well. Their position as international carriers had by the mid-seventeenth century become too predominant to be long maintained. Other states were certain to attempt to shake it by developing their own merchant marines; the Navigation System which developed in England from the 1650s onwards (see p. 134) was merely the most successful of a number of restrictive measures directed by various governments against the Dutch. Yet their commercial decline was slow. They remained throughout the eighteenth century one of the greatest trading powers of Europe. But even in the trade of the Baltic, the branch of European commerce which they had dominated most completely in the previous century, they were now being supplanted, above all by Britain. Of the 845 ships which in 1790 sailed from Memel through the Sound to ports in western Europe, for example, 214 were bound for London; only 22 were destined for Amsterdam. From early in the century Britain also dominated the trade of St. Petersburg, though the Dutch were still in a leading position in that of the less important Baltic ports of Riga, Pillau, and Königsberg. In part this Dutch commercial decline was the result of the smallness of the population and resources of the United Provinces, which made it difficult for them to sustain large-scale industry and become really large importers and exporters on their own account. Their trade, always largely a carrying and entrepôt one, was thus especially vulnerable to the envy and restrictive commercial policies of other European states. Moreover the Dutch empire in what is now Indonesia, though valuable, never gave rise to a trade as large as that of Britain and France with their American and Caribbean colonies; and the rigidity of Dutch commercial policy, seen in the continuance until 1795 of the trading monopoly of the Dutch East India Company and the failure in 1738 and 1751 of proposals to make Amsterdam a free port, may have helped to accentuate the decline.

France, the third great commercial state of western Europe, occupied in some ways a position intermediate between those of Britain and the Dutch. Her seaborne trade never seriously challenged that of Britain in scale. It was very vulnerable to British attack in time of war and during the first half of the century it grew only slightly. On the other hand the years between the peace of 1763 and the outbreak of the Revolution saw a very striking increase in French colonial trade, above all with the sugar islands of the West Indies, and the consolidation of France's commercial dominance in much of the Mediterranean.

By comparison with those of Britain, France, and the Dutch

Republic every other merchant marine in Europe was of secondary importance. Hamburg had now emerged as, after London and Amsterdam, the greatest commercial and financial centre in northern Europe. She was one of the free ports which played a great role in international exchanges during this period and which often had highly cosmopolitan populations. But she was essentially an entrepôt; and her own shipping, though not insignificant, was tiny by comparison with that of the great western states. Genoa was still a commercial centre of some significance. So was Venice, but her merchant marine was now in rapid decline—the British minister reported in 1765 that for many years she had sent no ships to any destination west of Malta for fear of the Barbary corsairs of north Africa, who remained throughout the century a considerable threat to the shipping of states with small navies. The very substantial trade of Naples and Leghorn (both of them also free ports) owed its existence to British, French, and to a lesser extent Dutch ships, while in the ports of the Iberian peninsula foreign vessels greatly outnumbered those of Spain and Portugal. The seaborne trade of the Ottoman Empire was in the hands of Greeks, Jews, Armenians, and above all the colonies of west European merchants to be found in all the major ports of the sultan's dominions; it too was carried on in French, British, Dutch, or, later in the century, Austrian or Russian ships. Sweden and Denmark were commercial powers of some importance in northern Europe, and Prussia had some merchant marine though nearly all its ships were small and suitable only for relatively short-distance trade; but Russia, like the Ottoman Empire, depended overwhelmingly on the west European states for the carriage of her imports and exports. For most of the century the superiority of western to eastern Europe was more marked in maritime trade than in volume of industrial production.

This superiority was important because the carriage of heavy or bulky goods by land for any distance was almost impossibly difficult and expensive. In England main roads improved considerably during the century in a rather haphazard way, through the creation of numerous turnpike trusts. In France a number of great administrators, above all Daniel Trudaine, who controlled the building of roads and bridges by the central government in the period 1743–69, had endowed the country by the time of the Revolution with a system of highways radiating from Paris which were unequalled anywhere. But in the rest of Europe little was done to improve even the most important roads; and everywhere minor and secondary roads remained appallingly bad. It is important, moreover, to remember that the cost of land transport could fluctuate sharply as a result of good or bad harvests. Horses and mules consumed hay, oats, barley, and other fodder crops. A poor harvest meant expensive food for animals as well as men and thus a level of freight charges which might temporarily cripple all landborne trade.

The rivers, relatively cheap and accessible means of transport, were all too often made expensive and difficult to use by the tolls and customs duties levied on traffic. Thus on the Rhine between Kehl and the Dutch frontier, because of the political fragmentation of western Germany, there were reckoned to be about thirty customs barriers. Even within the boundaries of a single state the position could be as bad or worse. At the beginning of the reign of Louis XV there were nearly 5,700 privately-owned tolls, used by their owners as a source of income, on French roads and rivers. In the middle of the century it was alleged that a boatman taking a load of staves from Lorraine to Languedoc had to stop twenty-two times to pay thirty-eight different tolls and duties. The sweeping away of these fantastically complex barriers to France's internal trade had been proposed as early as the mid-sixteenth century; but not until 1790–1, in the death-agony of the old régime, was it possible to achieve it. In Spain there was a customs barrier between Castile and Valencia until 1717, while Andalusia retained her own customs system until 1778. Moreover Spain, like France and Germany, suffered from the complete lack of a unified national system of weights and measures. Tuscany, under the rule of the last Medici Grand Dukes in the early decades of the century, was divided, almost incredibly, by no fewer than 187 customs barriers of different kinds. The Habsburg dominions were for much of this period divided into six separate customs areas and the abolition of the most important barrier to internal free trade, that between Hungary and the rest of the monarchy, was not even proposed until 1781. One of the few real economic advantages enjoyed by eighteenth-century Russia over many other European states was that the use of her great rivers was unimpeded by tolls and that her weights, measures, currency, and legal system were more or less effectively unified. The gross inefficiency of Europe's land communications meant that areas geographically far apart could be in close touch with each other by sea while others separated by a relatively short land journey might have little contact. It was easier, for example, to send goods from Bordeaux to Haiti than from Bordeaux to Paris. The economics of transport were thus highly favourable to a small island state such as Britain and correspondingly unfavourable to the great territorial empires of Russia and Austria.

In financial organization, as in many other aspects of economic life, progress was concentrated within a few parts of western Europe. The Dutch Republic remained in many ways the financial centre of the continent. It was much the greatest exporter of capital. In 1776 Lord North, the British prime minister, alleged (though with considerable exaggeration) that three-sevenths of the National Debt was in Dutch hands; and there were few parts of Europe in which Dutch money was not active in some way during the century. Amsterdam, though more and more challenged by London, remained the greatest European centre of international borrowing, of bullion-broking, and perhaps of marine insurance. In Britain a range of new national financial institutions—the Bank of England, the Bank of Scotland, the National Debt—was developing. A banking mechanism (private banks in England, more stable joint-stock ones in Scotland) was slowly and sometimes painfully emerging and helping to place the nation's resources at the service of its growing trade, industry, and agriculture. By 1800 there were about seventy private banks in London alone, though until late in the century their scarcity in the provinces made it often surprisingly difficult to remit money from one provincial centre to another. There was an increasing flow of British investment abroad, above all to the Western Hemisphere; in 1797, when the prime minister, the younger William Pitt, attempted to calculate the likely yield of the new income-tax, he estimated Britain's income from this source at five million pounds.

In France financial mechanisms were much less developed than in Britain or the United Provinces. Most substantial French merchants performed some of the functions of bankers, buying and selling drafts on each other and creating credit. But not until the reign of Napoleon I was there a national central bank; and large-scale financial dealings tended to revolve around government loans and contracts rather than investment in trade or industry. The key to success as a financier in eighteenth-century Paris was influence at court. The position was not altogether different in London, where subscription to government loans, sometimes on very lucrative terms, was normally confined to a small group of favoured bankers and merchants. But the importance of good official contacts was much greater in France. There, as a recent historian has pointed out, 'the most spectacular operations of old régime capitalism were made possible by royal finance and political manipulation rather than industrial or maritime enterprise'. Moreover the whole climate of opinion in France was distrustful of large-scale finance in a way that was ceasing to be true of Britain and had for long been unknown in the United Provinces. Religious influences still inspired hostility to the practice of lending money at interest, which continued to be condemned, at least in theory, by the Papacy (though inhibitions of this kind were less marked in France than in Spain and some parts of Italy). In the speculative mania of 1719–20, the 'Mississippi Bubble', thousands of Frenchmen had suffered loss in an unprecedented burst of hysteria produced by currency inflation and hopes of great profits to be made in trade with the French colonies. This episode left an enduring legacy of distrust of paper money and large-scale financial organization. Reinforced by the currency inflation during the Revolution, it was to impede the development of French financial life until far into the nineteenth century.

Elsewhere in Europe there was little advanced financial organization except in a number of city-republics such as Genoa (now in relative decline in this respect), Hamburg, Frankfurt, Geneva, and to a lesser extent Zürich and Berne. The great military-bureaucratic states of central and eastern Europe continued to lag far behind in this respect. Shortage of capital, lack of expertise in large-scale financial dealings and of a suitably capitalist mental atmosphere, meant that efforts to found state banks in both Prussia and the Habsburg dominions had little effective result. In Russia conditions were if anything even more unfavourable. Under Catherine II the Russian government achieved from the 1770s onwards the distinction of being the first major power to maintain a paper currency with reasonable success over a long period; not until the early 1790s did the paper rouble begin to depreciate sharply in terms of the silver one. But this success was an index rather of the strength of the central government and of the country's relative isolation from the mainstream of European economic life than of anything else. The financial structures of Poland and the Ottoman Empire were even more primitive than those of the other east and central European states. Only in a few western areas of the continent could there be found both substantial amounts of liquid capital and relatively efficient mechanisms for its investment.

The essential conservatism of European economic life is seen most clearly of all in the predominant importance of agriculture. The city-states of Germany and Switzerland and the Dutch provinces of Holland and Friesland were almost the only political units in Europe in which the cultivation of the soil was not the most important economic activity. Even in Britain at the beginning of this period probably less than 13 per cent. of the population lived in towns of 5,000 or more people; by 1800 the proportion had risen to 25 per cent., but agriculture was still the most important element in economic life. In France in the 1790s a very well-informed observer estimated that only 31 per cent. of the national income was derived from trade and industry and the rest from land. The figure was no more than an educated guess but it is probably fairly near the truth. Almost everywhere east of the Rhine the importance of agriculture was overwhelming.

Agriculture in eighteenth-century Europe varied very widely in its techniques and productivity and in its social organization and influence. In some western areas a dense population, adequate supplies of capital and technical knowledge, and relatively good communications encouraged efficiency and large-scale production for the market. Such were most of the Netherlands, much of the south-east and Midlands of England, to a lesser extent some parts of France such as Normandy.

In the Netherlands the production of cash crops such as madder, woad, flax, and hops had already been considerably developed in the seventeenth century; in the eighteenth, agriculture there continued to be the most commercialized and productive in Europe. In parts of England technical improvements were becoming marked by the 1720s. New crops such as turnips and clover were being cultivated. Stock was being improved by selective breeding. New tools such as the horse-hoe and the seed-drill were coming into use. Slowly farms were becoming larger, a prerequisite of greater technical efficiency. Small freeholders, the yeomen of tradition and political mythology, were giving way to tenant farmers who cultivated on a larger scale. Throughout the century, especially after about 1760, common lands were being enclosed and age-old common rights of pasture and of fuel-gathering in woodlands were being lost to village communities. In France also interest in technical improvement was growing in the later decades of the century, at least among the nobility and the more well-to-do farmers, while a movement for the enclosure of common lands, woods, and wastes, was gathering strength. A series of royal edicts in 1767–71 allowed enclosure of this kind in almost all the French provinces. And in all these relatively advanced parts of western Europe there was now a considerable technical literature on agricultural problems; in England the first works on the cultivation of clover and the potato had been published as early as the 1660s.

The scope and completeness of this agricultural improvement can easily be exaggerated. The highly capitalized and efficient farms of East Anglia and parts of the Midlands contrasted strikingly with those in Wales, and still more with those in the

Scottish Highlands, where as late as the 1840s a tenant's holding in parts of Argyll and Inverness-shire often still consisted of separate and unconsolidated strips. In France peasant resistance to change of any kind—for example to the introduction of the potato—was very strong. The efforts of agricultural societies and of Louis XVI himself to improve techniques by setting up model farms and offering prizes for agricultural improvements had little effect. Indeed the better-off peasant, precisely because he had some stake in the existing agrarian structure, often proved more hostile to change than the poor peasant or labourer who had little or nothing to lose by it.

Elsewhere in Europe technical innovation was usually unimportant or unknown and the position of the cultivator tended to depend very much on whether large-scale production for the market was a practical proposition. Where it was, as in much of Poland and Prussia which exported grain to western Europe, above all through the great port of Danzig, and perhaps also in the Baltic provinces of Russia, there was a marked tendency, already clearly visible in the previous century, for landlords to tighten their hold on their peasants and exploit them more intensively in order to produce more for sale. In these areas the economic opportunities created by the growth of urban markets, which in England or the Netherlands meant technical advance and greater productive efficiency, led merely to increasingly heavy burdens on the serf and a worsening of his position. The Prussian, Polish, or Russian landowner, faced with these opportunities, met them, understandably enough, by using to the full his one economic asset—a supply of cheap serf labour. All over eastern Europe, notably in Russia under the aegis of the Imperial Free Economic Society, there was discussion of the necessity for improving methods of cultivation and a slowly growing understanding of the undesirable social and intellectual side-effects of serfdom. But change was inhibited by lack of capital and technical knowledge, and above all by timidity, conservatism, and the refusal of the landowning class to surrender control of its peasants.

Between the extremes of eastern and western Europe there were large areas in which agrarian conditions remained remarkably stable. In much of west and south Germany poor communications and the lack of large accessible markets meant that there was little incentive to form large estates. There the position of the peasant, who was often also a part-time industrial worker under the domestic system, remained relatively secure. In Spain and Italy stability, or rather stagnation, of a less desirable kind could be seen. Though Sicily had long ceased to be the greatest grain-exporting area of Europe, as she had been during much of the sixteenth century, this led to no improvement in the position of her peasantry, who remained one of the most depressed to be found anywhere. Castile was still only slowly recovering from the prostration of the later seventeenth century; her scanty population helped to keep her agriculture backward and unproductive. In Aragon, where seigneurial rights were much more oppressive, the lord's control over his peasants was reduced by an important decree of 1716 which vested all criminal jurisdiction in the crown. But this made no change in the economic structure of the Aragonese countryside or in agricultural organization and methods. In Sweden the sparseness of the population helped to slow the pace of advance, in spite of the efforts of a number of innovating noble landowners; while in Denmark efforts to restrict serfdom had disappointing practical results. Not until much later was Danish agriculture to become a model for the rest of Europe.

Agricultural change was thus the exception rather than the rule. Where it did take place its social as distinct from its economic results could be actively harmful, as in the intensification of serfdom over much of the eastern half of the continent. The dominance of the European economy by an agriculture so resistant to change was merely the most obvious illustration of the essential conservatism, at least until very late in the century, of economic life in general.

Economic ideas, however, were developing quite rapidly. In this respect the first half of the century was dominated by 'mercantilism'. This current of ideas took varying forms in different countries and the economic literature it produced was extensive rather than profound. All its adherents, however, emphasized state power rather than the wealth or happiness of the individual as the chief objective of economic policy. All assumed that political and economic power were necessarily interdependent, and that states must always compete with each other for markets and economic resources. All tended to stress problems of production and consumption and to ignore those of distribution. This attitude was increasingly challenged from the 1750s onwards. In France the group of thinkers usually known as the Physiocrats—Turgot, the Marquis de Mirabeau, Dupont de Nemours, Quesnay (court physician to Louis XV and their leader in so far as they had one)—rejected completely the mercantilist stress on the importance of industry. To them land was the ultimate source of all wealth, industry and trade merely secondary and parasitic forms of economic activity. More important, they emphasized heavily the idea of a natural economic order, both between states and between different interests within a single state. This was to be attained by freeing economic life from artificial restrictions and giving greater liberty of action to the individual. The Physiocrats differed considerably among themselves, though unlike the believers in mercantilism they were a small, intellectual, and self-conscious group whose activities were concentrated within a time-span of little more than two decades. But the difference between the two currents of thought is fundamental; and the Physiocrats, unlike any of their predecessors, consciously attempted to formulate a science of economics, a body of doctrines which described and explained economic activity as a whole. They were not content, as virtually all mercantilist writers had been, to discuss merely specific, limited, and practical problems. To them, as to none of their precursors, economics was more than applied economics.

Both their emphasis on the freedom of the individual as a necessity of the wellbeing of society and their attempt to construct a general science of economics were carried further and systematized by Adam Smith in his *Wealth of Nations* (1776), one of the key books of the century. By the 1780s his attack on restrictive trade systems had begun to arouse a response in the governing circles of both Britain and France, one which was embodied in the remarkably liberal Anglo-French commercial treaty of 1786. As far as merchants and the general public were concerned, however, it was only in Britain that Free Trade ideas had begun to take root by the end of the century; and even there what was being demanded was the freeing of individual branches of trade rather than of trade in general. In particular the elaborate system of Corn Laws was now beginning to come under fire, so that in 1790 the Glasgow Chamber of Commerce can be found demanding the 'repeal of the whole system of Corn Laws, and the establishment of a perfect freedom of trade in that essential necessary of life'. Even in Britain the demand for true Free Trade was still in embryo; but it was an embryo which was to grow and ripen with enormous results over the next two generations.

Colonial trade, banking and finance, economic ideas, above all, in some areas, industry—these were the developing aspects of Europe's economic life in the eighteenth century. But in the main they were confined to parts, usually small ones, of western Europe. In most cases they influenced directly only a small minority of the population even there. The dominance of agriculture; the unimportance of towns; the shortage of capital; the poorness of communications; the slow diffusion of technical knowledge—all these discouraged progress over most of the continent. So did other and more subtle factors. There was a striking lack of the most elementary knowledge of the facts of economic life. Few governments (that of Sweden was perhaps the only important exception) knew with any exactitude the size of the populations they ruled. Almost as few had any idea what the balance of trade or payments of their territories was at any given moment. The economic world was not yet being subjected to the close analysis and quantitative description which were more and more being applied to the physical one. Thinking about commercial problems could still be influenced by the totally unscientific idea of the 'just price', financial life still impeded by a prejudice against taking interest on loans. Even in France, which now led the world in the development of mathematics, the annuity loans by which the American War of 1778–83 was partly financed made no allowance at all for the age of the annuitant; so that an annuity bought on the life of a child could easily yield a return, over time, of as much as five times the purchase price. This is a startling illustration of the slowness with which common sense, let alone science, was applied to economic issues even in the more advanced European states.

Over most of Europe men still lived in an economic and social world dominated by the past. It was changing. But even after the cataclysm of the French Revolution the changes were slow over the greater part of the continent; before 1789 they were even slower, to many Europeans almost imperceptible.

# 4
## Monarchs and Governments

THE EIGHTEENTH CENTURY, almost as much as the seventeenth, was an age of kings. All the greatest European states
were monarchies. The internal politics of most of them, at the
highest level, revolved around struggles between competing
factions for access to the ruler and influence over him. International relations were deeply and sometimes disastrously
influenced by the conflicting dynastic claims of ruling families,
claims which underlay the wars of succession which bulk so
large in the history of the period.

It was taken for granted by most contemporaries that
hereditary monarchy was the most natural and therefore the
most effective of all forms of rule. The time-worn analogy
which likened the relations between king and people to those
between a father and his children had still real meaning to
ordinary men and women all over Europe. In particular it was
assumed that monarchy was the only type of régime which
could rule efficiently a large state or one which was expanding
rapidly. Of course kings could be selfish, lazy, or weak. They
could give their confidence to the wrong ministers and wantonly
disregard the interests of their subjects. Nevertheless in
eighteenth-century Europe strong monarchy seemed the prerequisite of a powerful state and the main engine of progress.

These beliefs were fully justified. Only small, territorially
static, and sometimes decaying states, such as the republics of
Venice and Genoa and the Swiss cantons, could afford to dis-
pense with hereditary monarchy. The most obviously expand-

ing ones, Russia and Prussia, as well as such traditional great powers as France and Spain, possessed monarchies which were extremely powerful in theory and to varying extents in practice. Britain was unique in being able to increase her territory and international importance while slowly weakening her monarchy; and even in British political life the ruler played an extremely important part until after the end of this period. Above all there was plenty of evidence to suggest that a weak monarchy was likely to prove disastrous to any state. In the United Provinces the forty or more years of republican dominance which followed the death of William III of Orange in 1702 coincided with a marked decline in the international importance of the federation and a disastrous collapse of its military and naval strength. William IV, who was brought to power as Stadholder and Captain-General in 1747, when the Provinces seemed about to be overwhelmed by French invasion, and William V, who succeeded him in 1751, were hopelessly weak rulers. Heavily handicapped by its archaic constitution and by the endemic rivalry between Orangists and Republicans, which at the end of the 1780s seemed to have brought the country to the verge of civil war, the United Provinces appeared a textbook case of the evils in store for any state which tried to do without a strong hereditary monarchy. In the same way the weakening of royal power in Sweden by the constitution of 1720 seemed to most contemporaries, not unfairly, the most important reason for the internal divisions and international ineffectiveness which marked the country's history for the next half-century. Above all Poland offered a striking warning of what could happen to a state deprived of the leadership which powerful monarchy alone could give. The weakness of the Polish monarchy, the conflicts, pressures, and factional struggles which accompanied the election of new rulers in 1697, 1733, and 1764, were one of the aspects of the country's decline which most impressed foreigners. Its position as a mere 'crowned republic' contrasted startlingly with that in its great neighbours, Russia and Prussia. Clearly their progress at its expense was to be explained largely by the immensely greater power of their rulers as compared with the increasingly helpless kings of Poland.

Moreover almost everywhere where monarchy was weak or non-existent, as in Poland, Venice, and to a lesser extent Sweden and even the Dutch provinces, society tended to be stagnant, and administration, the judiciary, and even economic life dominated by tradition and group privilege. In the great monarchies, by contrast, there was always at least the possibility that an intelligent and determined ruler would be able to override tradition, disregard the past, and use his authority to introduce necessary changes in many aspects of his people's lives. This was what Peter I of Russia had attempted, very spectacularly and with partial success. It was what the 'Enlightened Despots' of the second half of the century were to attempt by different and gentler methods. Monarchy in eighteenth-century Europe was not in general a progressive institution; but it had potentialities for progress far greater than any possessed by the churches, the aristocracies, or the other privileged groups which dominated European society.

To the overwhelming majority of Europeans, then, kingship was the most desirable form of government, indeed the only conceivable one. Kingship differed greatly, however, in different parts of the continent, and thus reflected the social, economic, and above all historical differences between the great states. At one extreme stood Russia. There the powers of the ruler were unlimited in theory and very great in practice. This was because there was no group or institution in the country which could oppose him with any hope of success or indeed which wished to do so. Peter I had effectively transformed the Russian nobility into a class of hereditary, though often reluctant, state servants, and by giving noble status and privileges to great numbers of foreigners and Russians of relatively humble origins had largely deprived the nobility of what sense of unity it still retained. Henceforth a *noblesse* of the west European type, a class deriving its importance largely from its lineage and noble ancestry, could not exist in Russia. In 1730 the complete failure of an attempt by a group of great nobles to remodel the régime as a noble oligarchy, and in particular the failure of the great majority of the *dvoryanstvo* to support the attempt, illustrated this point. The events of that year showed that noble

obstruction of the processes of government (as distinct from
mere palace revolutions) was not now a serious danger to any
ruler of Russia. The church too had been reduced to subservience by Peter, a subservience symbolized by the fact that
from the coronation of the Empress Elizabeth in 1742 onwards
all rulers of Russia crowned themselves in the Cathedral of the
Dormition in the Kremlin, the senior Russian Archbishop
merely handing them the crown. The Tsar Paul, at his coronation in 1797, even gave himself communion, though this
assertion of independence of all priestly authority remained
unique. The impotence of the church in Russia to oppose the
monarchy was driven home most effectively of all by the
secularization of most of its landed property in 1764. Municipal,
provincial, or regional privileges of the kind so common in
western and central Europe were far less significant in Russia.
Central political institutions of course there were. A council
composed of ministers, great officials, and court favourites
continued to exist throughout the century for the formulation
of policy. In 1718–19 Peter I had created a number of administrative colleges, each charged with the supervision of one
important field of government activity; some of these, notably
the Colleges for War and Foreign Affairs, remained very
important to the end of this period. The Senate which Peter
had set up in 1711 to supervise the workings of the whole
government machine continued to function, though increasingly
as a purely judicial institution. But the ruler was under no obligation to act through any of these bodies or even to consult them.
They existed, in the last analysis, as extensions of his will and
nothing more. The personal and arbitrary nature of his power
was underlined by the fact that until well into the nineteenth
century the chaotic mass of Russian legislation remained completely uncodified. The effective powers of the Russian monarchy, in other words, were limited less by social pressures or
legal rights than by merely physical factors—the size of the
country, the scantiness of its population, the poorness of its
communications. 'In all countries ruled by an unlimited power,'
wrote a Russian commentator in the mid-nineteenth century,
'there have always been and are some class, estate, some traditional

institutions, which in certain instances compel the sovereign to act in a certain way and set limits to his caprice; nothing of the sort exists in Russia.' This was at least as true a century earlier. It was this terrible simplicity of Russia's political and social institutions that made her monarchy unique in Europe.

The monarchy of Brandenburg-Prussia, though in some ways highly autocratic, particularly in the early decades of the century, was in practice far less absolute than that of Russia. Frederick William I, as has already been pointed out, had created an important structure of centralized administration, represented locally by the new Kriegs- und Domänenkammern and in Berlin above all by the Generaldirektorium established at the end of 1722. By temperament Frederick William I was a true autocrat. He had no conception of the state as something distinct from his own person; and neither the nobility nor the towns of Prussia were able to oppose him effectively. Nor did they wish to do so. But institutions inherited from the past, the Geheime Rat and the Regierungen, were still able to act to some extent as brakes upon his personal power. More important, the estates which continued to exist in parts of his dominions, traditional pseudo-representative bodies dominated by the nobility, could not be completely disregarded. Under his son, Frederick II (1740–86), the Prussian monarchy became somewhat more restricted in its powers, more 'constitutional'. Frederick was the first ruler of Brandenburg-Prussia to realize that the state existed independently of its ruler and that its interests did not necessarily coincide with his. The last decade of his reign saw a steady movement towards consolidating the rule of law in Prussia, towards giving the highest judicial organs greater independence and enabling them to act as both a link and a buffer between the ruler and his subjects. This movement, which owed something to the ideas of Montesquieu (see pp. 114–15) culminated in the compilation of the great legal code, the Prüssisches Landrecht, of 1791.

In France the monarchy was, in theory, more powerful than in Prussia; in practice it was much weaker and its weakness grew as the century went on. There was little theoretical limit to the powers of the kings of France. They alone possessed

supreme legislative authority. The army and navy owed obedience and loyalty to them and not to such an abstraction as the
French state. They could override the decisions of any court of
law. No elected or representative body could dictate their
policies or interfere with their choice of ministers. But their
effective authority was far less than the theory indicated. A
country so great, populous, and varied as France could not now
be governed as traditional theory envisaged except by a man of
exceptional energy and determination. For such a one personal
rule was still possible, as Napoleon I was to show. But Louis XV
and Louis XVI were very far from being Napoleons. Weak,
timid, and increasingly out of touch with the life and feeling
of their subjects, they had neither the will nor the capacity to
play effectively their traditional role. 'The king,' wrote the
Emperor Joseph II after a visit to Paris in 1777, 'is absolute
only in his power to pass from one slavery to another. He can
change his ministers, but unless he is a transcendent genius he
can never be master of the conduct of affairs.' The administrative machinery of eighteenth-century France was in many ways
highly efficient by the standards of that period. But its efficiency
was the work of able ministers in Paris and energetic and public-
spirited officials in the provinces. The monarchs of the period
contributed nothing to it.

Moreover even able rulers would have found it an uphill
struggle to assert their authority effectively. This was because
French society was now an agglomeration of privileged bodies
whose power had been increased by the minority which followed the death of Louis XIV. The provincial estates were now
a real force only in two provinces, Dauphiné and Brittany.
Elsewhere they had long ceased to exist or had been reduced to
impotence. The church on the other hand still retained great
privileges, above all in matters of taxation, which impeded
administrative improvement and effective concentration of
power in the hands of the ruler. Privileged towns, guilds, even
universities, the whole complex and irrational structure of
traditional society, set limits to the power of the government
which only popular revolution proved strong enough to override. Most important of all, the *parlements*, the dozen or so

mainly hereditary legal corporations which functioned as
courts of appeal and also possessed great administrative importance, became steadily more obstructive in their attitude to the
central government as the century progressed. As early as 1720
the Parlement of Paris, by far the most powerful of them, had
been exiled from the capital for a time because of its opposition
to essential financial legislation. In 1749–51, in a struggle
which may have decided the fate of the *ancien régime* in France,
the *parlements*, backed by the church and much of the nobility,
successfully resisted a series of efforts to introduce new and
desperately needed taxation. When the chancellor Maupeou
once more exiled the Parlement of Paris in 1771 and abolished
the offices held by its members it seemed that the monarchy
might still shake off this dangerous incubus. But in 1774 the
accession of Louis XVI brought Maupeou's fall and the restora-
tion of the *status quo*. Henceforth, until the crisis which pre-
cipitated the Revolution, the *parlements* represented the most
conservative aspects of French political and social life. From the
1760s, moreover, they tended more and more to work in concert. Increasingly they claimed to be each a component part of
a single great institution which provided the only real bulwark
against unrestrained royal despotism and, in some sense at
least, represented the interests of the French people against
those of the ruler. Such claims were ridiculous. The *parlements*
stood not for liberty but for traditional and class privileges of a
kind more and more difficult to justify. Yet for all their falsity
these claims aroused some response from French public
opinion.

In France, then, the greatest of European monarchies was
struggling vainly with domestic opposition. Because of the
weakness of Louis XV and XVI it was more and more taking
the line of least resistance and surrendering to its opponents.
In Spain and above all in the Habsburg dominions the rulers
faced much more powerful and more deeply entrenched opposition. In both, monarchs struggled to unify their territories more
effectively, to centralize and improve the machinery of government, to collect more taxes and beat down the class and
regional privileges which impeded political progress. In Spain

Philip V, taking advantage of the hostility of the Catalans during the war of the Spanish Succession, in 1714 destroyed the formerly great privileges of Catalonia. This has sometimes been taken as marking the beginning of modern Spanish history. Simultaneously the Cortes (parliament) of Aragon ceased to meet; and though those of Castile and Navarre continued to exist they no longer counted for much. Spain was still far from being completely unified, politically or otherwise. In particular the Basque provinces of the north retained a highly privileged position, notably with regard to taxation. But she was now more effectively united and subject to her rulers than ever before. The new state of affairs was symbolized by the reorganization of the administrative system (see p. 6) in the early years of the century. It is true that Philip V, at least after the first years of his reign, cut a very poor figure indeed; but Charles III (1759–88), who continued and intensified the reforming impulses of the first decades of the century, was with all his limitations the best and most effective king Spain had seen for two hundred years.

The rulers of the Habsburg Empire confronted difficulties much greater than those that the kings of France or Spain had to cope with. Their territories, sprawling over most of central Europe with outlying possessions in Milan, the southern Netherlands, and (until 1735) in Naples, were impossible to govern effectively in eighteenth-century conditions (see pp. 11–12). In no sense—linguistic, economic, historical, or administrative—did they form a unit. It was impossible to transform them into a centralized state. Nevertheless the second half of the eighteenth century saw a remarkable series of struggles to modernize and rationalize their administration. In the first decade of the reign of Charles VI (1711–40) there were considerable though unsuccessful efforts to improve the chaotic financial structure which so greatly handicapped every ruler of the Habsburg Empire in this period. These were followed by more than two decades of stagnation and even decline; but the bitter rivalry with Prussia, which began in 1740, and the shock of the loss of Silesia, were a very effective incentive to change. The army was enlarged and improved, drilled and uniformed on the

Prussian model, and provided with a rudimentary general staff. To pay for these changes the yield of taxation had to be increased; and this was done, notably by a series of financial reforms introduced by Count Haugwitz in 1748. The control of the estates over taxation was reduced in many of the provinces, and Maria Theresa attempted, though without much success, to weaken the separatism of Hungary by calling meetings of its diet as seldom as possible. (It met only three times during the forty years of her reign.) Something was done to break down the grossly privileged position with regard to taxation which the nobility and the Catholic church had hitherto enjoyed, while new agencies of the central government, Räprasentationen and Kammern, were established in a number of provinces. In particular there was an important overhaul of local government in Bohemia in 1751. The growth of the bureaucracy which all these developments involved slowly created what the Empire had hitherto conspicuously lacked—an important social group with a real stake in the growth of a powerful centralized monarchy. New central institutions were created—a state chancery for Foreign Affairs in 1742, a united chancery for Austria and Bohemia in 1749, a Council of State in 1760.

This slow, painful, and uneven movement towards administrative unity continued under Maria Theresa's son, Joseph II (1780–90). Joseph, the classical example of an 'enlightened despot', almost the only ruler of a major eighteenth-century state really to merit the title, spent his reign in wholehearted efforts to develop and improve his territories. These won him the bitter dislike of a large part of his subjects and ended in at least partial failure. His attempt to make German the administrative language of all his central European possessions aroused alarm and hostility in Hungary and some other provinces. His refusal to be crowned King of Hungary in the traditional way and his removal to Vienna of the crown of St. Stephen, the symbol of Hungarian nationhood, did even more to inflame Magyar feeling against him. So did the extension of military conscription to Hungary in 1784 and his efforts to sweep away the immunity from direct taxation which the Hungarian nobility and church had hitherto enjoyed. In the Austrian

Netherlands, itself a group of provinces each with its own archaic and irrational institutions, his well-meant efforts at modernization and his hostility to clerical privileges had produced by the end of his reign open revolt and the temporary collapse of his authority. Almost alone among eighteenth-century rulers he sincerely wished to change and improve the social structure of the territories he ruled. In particular he continued and intensified the efforts which his mother had made to improve the lot of the peasantry in his dominions, though in this he was inspired by considerations of utility and efficiency rather than by humanitarianism. A great decree of 1781 abolished personal serfdom throughout the Habsburg Empire (though not the labour-services—*robot*—which the peasants normally owed to their lords). Other decrees limited the right of the lord to punish his peasants and in 1789 introduced the most radical scheme of taxation reform envisaged in any major state during this period.

Yet this remarkable reign closed in an atmosphere of failure and defeat. As early as 1785 the growing unpopularity of his régime had forced Joseph to begin a large-scale reorganization of the police system in his dominions, and newspaper censorship was set up early in 1790. The war with Turkey which broke out in 1788 was bitterly unpopular, especially because of the demands for recruits and supplies which it imposed on the peasantry in parts of the monarchy. Joseph's religious policies (see p. 121) roused considerable opposition; and the taxation reform of 1789, combined with events in France, stimulated demands, though as yet only from a small radical minority in some of the cities, for the abolition of all forms of feudalism. In the last days of his life, therefore, Joseph found himself forced to withdraw some of the most unpopular of his reforms. His brother and successor, the equally remarkable Leopold II, attempted to continue, more tactfully and discreetly, many of his brother's policies. But the fears aroused by the French Revolution meant that his death in 1792 was followed by a period of reaction and stagnation in the government of the Habsburg territories which did not end until 1848.

Joseph II's failure was in part the result of his own character, intolerant, dogmatic, hasty, and unrealistic. 'To do things by halves,' he had boasted to his mother, 'does not agree at all with my principles.' His energy and sincerity failed through their own excess. But he also failed because the history and above all the social structure of his dominions were against him. The privileged groups and institutions—the church, the nobility, the provincial estates—opposed him, sometimes violently. Groups favourable to radical change did exist in the Habsburg Empire, as the repercussions there of the French Revolution were to show. In the 1790s artisans in Vienna and a few other cities, a number of the Hungarian gentry, and small groups of intellectuals in different parts of the Empire, sympathized actively with events in France. But these forces were totally unable to threaten the *status quo*. Effective support Joseph received only from a relatively small number of high-ranking officials, men favourable by training and self-interest to his dream of administrative unity; and this proved too fragile and narrow a foundation for his schemes.

In Britain both monarchy and administration differed from those in any other major state. The most outstanding characteristic of the monarchy was the discrepancy, which widened steadily as the century progressed, between its theoretical and its real powers. In this respect it resembled that of France. But whereas the decline of the French monarchy meant a growing danger of chaos, the rulers of Britain were surrendering their powers, almost imperceptibly and sometimes unconsciously, to parliament and above all to the great new undefined institution of the cabinet. It was possible, therefore, for the weakening of the monarchy to be accompanied by a positive improvement in the efficiency of the central government. The extent to which the monarchy in Britain lost power during this period must not be exaggerated. The government was still the king's government; systematic and sustained opposition to it carried a flavour of disloyalty. It became virtually essential for the ministers whom the king had chosen to be able to command a majority in parliament. But the house of commons was elected on a very narrow franchise, especially the borough members who made up four-fifths of it; and voters were exceedingly unlikely to oppose any government known to possess royal approval. Not until far into the following century was such a government defeated at the polls. Until late in this period it was very difficult to force the ruler to accept policies which he opposed or ministers whom he disliked. As late as 1807 George III was able to bring down a ministry because of his refusal to agree to the grant of equal political rights to Catholics. Under George I (1714–27) and George II (1727–60) foreign policy and military affairs were regarded as spheres of government in which the king was particularly entitled to an important, indeed decisive, say.

Yet the real powers of the British monarchy were certainly less at the end of the eighteenth century than at its beginning. The Hanoverians had inherited the throne by virtue of an act of parliament, the Act of Settlement of 1701. They could not claim and never attempted to claim that they ruled by Divine Right, as the kings of France could and did. The prerogative powers which they inherited in 1714 were in a number of important ways less than those enjoyed by the Stuarts in the seventeenth century. Moreover the great wars fought against France from the end of the seventeenth century were expensive. Only parliament, by agreeing to the taxation required, could find the necessary amounts of money; inevitably this led to a growth of parliamentary concern with foreign affairs and an increase in the amount of information about them which parliament was given. Both George I and George II were at least as interested in their German electorate of Hanover as they were in Britain. The former perhaps never really understood British politics and the latter lacked the strength of character and the intelligence to utilize to the full his still very real powers. The result was that George III found on his accession in 1760 that the balance of power between the king and his ministers was now less favourable to the monarchy than ever before. This change had not been accompanied by a corresponding change in constitutional theory; the new king therefore attempted to assert in practice powers, especially with respect to his choice of ministers and control of policy, which were undoubtedly his by tradition. The attempt was complicated by the instability of British politics in the 1760s and defeated by the failure from 1775 onwards of the government led by Lord North (1770–82) to subdue the American colonies. For a short time in 1783 the king had even to accept a cabinet in which Charles James Fox, the Whig leader whom he feared and disliked most of all, played a leading role. Moreover the 'Economical Reform' legislation of 1782 was a deliberate effort by parliament to reduce the influence over some members and even over elections in a limited number of constituencies which the monarchy could still exert. In addition, by the end of the 1770s active popular discontent with the existing political system, notably in London itself and the great county of Yorkshire, was becoming serious. The County Associations formed in 1779–80 demanded a widening of the parliamentary suffrage and a redistribution of seats; and, though their activities were not directed against the monarchy as such, a more representative parliament was likely to prove the most serious of all obstacles to any future concentration of effective power in the hands of the king. In fact the movement rapidly collapsed in the summer of 1780; and though the demand for parliamentary reform lingered on for a decade any chance of its success was then destroyed for a generation by the French Revolution and its repercussions in England.

Nevertheless by the 1780s at the latest the monarchy in Britain was doomed to become eventually no more than a decorative appendage to the political life of the country. What was to inherit its powers was still unclear. The cabinet, comprising the holders of the main offices of state and the heads of all the great departments of government, had certainly emerged as a distinct institution by about 1740, and probably a good deal earlier. But it had no legal status whatever and remained for long completely lacking in unity. Its members were divided by personal rivalries and genuine differences over policy. Above all cabinets were divided because no political parties in the modern sense of the term existed, and ministers therefore represented merely small and often competing groups of M.P.s usually bound together by ties of patronage and family relationships. In particular the idea of a prime minister occupying a position clearly superior to that of his colleagues was widely resisted and

disliked. Not until the long tenure of office of the younger
William Pitt (1783–1801) did the principle of cabinet unity
begin to be effectively asserted and the country acquire its first
real prime minister. Moreover the fact that effectively organized
political parties still lay far in the future helped the king to
enjoy until late in the century very considerable freedom in the
choice of his ministers, and if necessary to play off one parliamentary faction against another.

The British monarchy, then, was unique during this period
in that it could work only in partnership with the one truly
powerful and respected representative body to be found in any
European state. It had no aura of divinity; it controlled only a
small bureaucracy and a weak and unpopular army. Nevertheless it was, like monarchy almost everywhere in Europe, an
institution both necessary and popular. Its real powers were
slowly evaporating. But this was a very gradual process and the
institutions and forces which were to inherit them were slow
to develop.

It is generally agreed that in the later eighteenth century,
notably in the generation from about 1760 to 1790, many of the
monarchies of Europe began to display new characteristics. In
one state after another rulers or ministers (Catherine II in
Russia, Frederick II in Prussia, Gustavus III in Sweden,
Charles III in Spain, Struensee in Denmark, Tanucci in Naples)
began to be influenced, or to claim that they were influenced,
by the ideas which economists and political philosophers, notably in France, had been proclaiming for several decades. This
'enlightened despotism' is in many ways an unsatisfactory
subject of study. Except in a few cases—notably those of the
Archduke Leopold in Tuscany (1765–90) and his better-known
brother Joseph in the Habsburg dominions—it was always
largely superficial and contrived. Usually the policies actively
pursued by the enlightened despots, however warm the welcome
they gave to new theories of government and administration,
ran to some extent in traditional channels.

All of them attempted to improve the administration of their
states, especially with regard to taxation, and to unify their

territories more effectively. Many of them attempted or at least envisaged judicial reforms, notably by the drawing up of elaborate legal codes. The code of civil procedure and the penal code issued by Joseph II in 1781 and 1787, and above all the great Prussian code of 1791, the outcome of many years of labour during the reign of Frederick II, are outstanding examples. With few exceptions the enlightened despots hoped to achieve their ends by increasing their own authority and the power of the central government in their states. But with the partial exception of the desire for legal reform none of these ambitions was new. In differing ways they had been seen in the activities of the 'New Monarchs' of the sixteenth century and in those of Louis XIV and his contemporaries; they were to be seen once more, with greater intensity and effect, in those of Napoleon I. Some elements of novelty can, it is true, be detected in the attitude of several rulers and governments of the later eighteenth century. In particular the growing humanitarianism, which 'enlightened' thought and writing had done much to foster, was now inspiring efforts to abolish judicial torture and greater consideration than in the past for the interests of such groups as orphans and old soldiers. But there were few rulers whose policies in practice represented more than the development of ambitions cherished by their predecessors. Thus Frederick II made little real alteration in the administrative system bequeathed him by his father; and most of his territorial ambitions, notably in Poland, were also inherited. Most of the changes which Catherine II attempted or contemplated in Russia—the secularization of church lands in 1764, the reform of local government in 1775, the codification of the law, attempted particularly by the unsuccessful Legislative Commission of 1767—had been suggested during the reigns of her predecessors. What distinguished Frederick and Catherine from Frederick William I and Peter the Great was not so much their policies as their explicit justification of them (especially in the case of Catherine) in terms of advanced contemporary thought. It was this appeal to intellectual and moral standards rather than to those of mere expediency that made these rulers appear to be doing something new. And this appeal was essentially spurious. No ruler of any major state could allow his policies to be dictated by theory, however attractive. The history, geographical position, and resources of the state he ruled, the power or weakness of its neighbours, and a host of other factors, set limits to what he might reasonably attempt in either internal or external affairs. Joseph II spent his reign in a continuous series of efforts to improve the administration of his territories and the condition of his subjects. More than any other major ruler of the period he was truly inspired by the theories of government then current in enlightened Europe. Yet his disregard of realities in his relations with the Hungarians, with the inhabitants of his Netherlands provinces, and with the Catholic church, and the failure and near-collapse to which this disregard had led by the end of his reign, were the supreme proof that, as always, there was an 'order of possible progress' in politics and all other aspects of life in the eighteenth century, and that this order could be disregarded only to a very limited extent.

In small states, with fewer international ambitions and usually a more homogeneous population, the position was easier. In them it was sometimes possible for an energetic ruler to introduce changes which would have been extremely difficult or dangerous in more important states. Thus the *impôt unique*, the single tax on land to replace all others, which was strongly advocated by the Physiocrats and was the most sweeping fiscal reform suggested during the century, was adopted only in the minor German state of Baden. It was in a small state, the Grand Duchy of Tuscany, that Leopold, the younger brother of Joseph II, attempted the most remarkable process of change from above to be seen anywhere in eighteenth-century Europe. Aided by two reforming ministers, Gianni and Tavanti, he freed agriculture and the grain trade, in 1766–75, from the generations-old legal restrictions that hampered their development. A new code of criminal law which he promulgated in 1786 was admired all over Europe. Unlike all his fellow rulers he made a real effort to associate his subjects with their government and to give at least a proportion of them some say in it. He is known to have been influenced by the political ideas and practice of the British American colonies, and on a visit to

Vienna in 1778-9 he severely criticized his brother's ideas as
'despotic and confused'. In a charter of 1782, which was never
effectively applied, he envisaged the establishment in Tuscany
of a central assembly, indirectly elected, with remarkably wide
powers. For a ruler voluntarily to surrender authority in this way
to a representative body was unparalleled, as were Leopold's
efforts to make Tuscany a perpetual neutral in European affairs,
disarmed and protected by an international guarantee in somewhat
the same way as Switzerland was to be in the nineteenth century.

But only in a minor state could enlightenment be pushed to
such lengths, and Leopold himself admitted that his reforming
schemes were made possible only by the smallness of Tuscany.
In no major state could the ideas of the Enlightenment have
more than a marginal effect on policy. Moreover it was possible
for reforming rulers or ministers to exist even where progressive
intellectual influences were very slight. There was no necessary
connexion between enlightened ideas and political progress.
Thus the Marques de Pombal, who for nearly three decades
(1750-77) dominated the government of Portugal, appears to
have owed little or nothing to the political theorists of the
period. Certainly no society in western Europe was less recep-
tive to new ideas than that of Portugal. Yet Pombal's energetic and often brutal efforts to break the power of the nobility
and the church, and his largely unsuccessful attempts to improve the economic life of Portugal, were in the mainstream of
'enlightened' practice. Spain under Charles III shows in a less
extreme form the same phenomenon of reforming impulses
largely divorced from direct connexion with enlightened
thought and applied in a highly conservative and traditional
society. Even in the Ottoman Empire, still almost immune to
European intellectual influences, there can be seen in the last
quarter of the century a slowly growing recognition, inspired
by defeat at the hands of Russia, of the need to improve on west
European lines the armed forces and perhaps other aspects of
the empire's life.

No régime, monarchical or not, could be more efficient than
the administrative system upon which it rested. All were limited

in practice by the many defects of eighteenth-century bureau-
cracies. Nearly all states, certainly all major ones, suffered from
a shortage of well-trained officials. Moreover government
offices, though not usually the most important ones, were sold
in large numbers in several states as a means of raising revenue.
Since they frequently thus became in a sense the private property of their holders they tended to escape from the control of
the ruler and his ministers and to be held by men with little
except money to recommend them. The sale of offices is still a
subject which awaits investigation on a European scale; and it is
clear that there were great divergencies in this respect between
different parts of the continent. The practice was widespread
in France, where the financial stringency of the last decades of
the reign of Louis XIV had given it wider currency than ever
before, and was known even in efficiency-minded Prussia. In
Russia on the other hand it never took root; and in some states,
notably Venice, it was difficult for the government to find buyers
even when it wished to sell official posts. Everywhere, however,
in the second half of the century, such sales were increasingly
regarded as an abuse to be avoided. In France, for example,
venal offices in the cities were abolished by an important edict
of 1764.

The administrative systems of pre-revolutionary Europe were
also weakened by a reliance, at least in their lower ranks, on
payment by fees rather than by fixed salaries. To the ordinary
man, especially if he became involved in legal proceedings of any
kind, this was often one of the most oppressive aspects of the
administration under which he lived. An official who might
have bought his post largely as a commercial speculation often
succumbed to the temptation to charge excessive fees for the
services he performed; or to make official procedures as complex
and slow-moving as possible in order to exact the maximum in
payments of this kind; or to supplement fees with bribes, since
the one imperceptibly shaded into the other. Moreover, since
society was in the main conservative and backward-looking,
bureaucracy was also except at the highest levels. Legal systems
in particular were resistant to change. Thus though the use of
torture for judicial purposes, the most repellent of all inherit-

ances from the past in legal matters, was under attack throughout the century it disappeared only very slowly. From about
1690 it ceased to be used in Britain; and it was virtually abolished in Prussia in 1740. But it was not until 1780–8 that it
was discarded in France; and it lingered on until 1798 in the
Dutch Republic, 1801 in Russia, and 1812 in Spain.

Above all, however, eighteenth-century administrations were
weakened by their lack of unified and rational organization. At
the highest level this was seen in the fact that specialized
ministries were still only in process of evolution. Thus in
Britain until 1782 the two secretaries of state (for the northern
and southern departments) continued to be responsible not
only for the conduct of foreign affairs but also for a very wide
and undefined range of domestic matters. In France the minister
for foreign affairs, in addition to his proper functions, controlled like other ministers the administration of a group of
provinces. In the same way, in the early part of the century the
Supreme War Council (Hofkriegsrat) in the Habsburg territories performed purely civil administrative and even judicial
functions as well as military and strategic ones. At a lower level
this lack of system was visible in the fact that many duties
which in a modern state would be performed by officials or
official bodies were still the responsibility of private individuals.
The outstanding example of this is the survival, over great
areas, of seigneurial lawcourts controlled by noble landowners
and constituting one of the most important expressions of their
feudal rights over their tenants. In France, where there were
still very many courts of this kind, it was estimated that the full-
and part-time judges employed in them before the Revolution
numbered from 70,000 to 80,000. In Brittany, one of the most
backward provinces, nine-tenths of all legal business was done
in these seigneurial courts and this escaped the royal judicial
system altogether. In Russia and Prussia also, much local
administration had as a matter of expediency to be delegated
by the government to the landowning class; and in a different
way the same thing happened in England, where the unpaid
and amateur justices of the peace, predominantly squires and
clergymen of the Church of England, performed not only

judicial functions but a wide variety of administrative ones. Indeed the seigneurial courts in France, with all the expense, complexity, and endless appeals which they involved, were superior to the local courts of Russia, Prussia, or even Britain in being staffed almost entirely by professional lawyers and not by amateurs chosen merely for their social position. In a few areas even such an essential public service as the postal system was still in the hands of private contractors until well into the eighteenth century. Thus in Piedmont, where it had for long been the monopoly of the Gonteri family, it did not fall under complete government control until 1720; and over a good deal of the Holy Roman Empire the posts continued to be directed, as they had been since the sixteenth century, by the Thurn und Taxis family, and in the Habsburg territories by the Paar family.

Above all, efficient administration was impeded by the existence over so much of Europe of an immensely complex structure of local, regional, and class privilege, particularly with regard to taxation. Variation between one province and another of the same state might be immense, so that in France for example an area subject to the *gabelle* (in effect an excise duty on salt) at the highest rate might pay nearly thirty times as much for this essential of life as one taxed at a lower rate. Over nearly all Catholic Europe the church paid less, sometimes very much less, than its share of taxes. In many states the nobility were favoured, often, as in Poland and Hungary, outrageously so; the willingness of the English landowners who controlled parliament to tax themselves with reasonable fairness was one of the foundations of British power during this period. The towns were often favoured at the expense of the countryside: this again was very marked in France, where municipal privileges were quite as indefensible as those of the church or nobility. A society so unfair and irrational could not, left to itself, produce a rational system of taxation. Yet without a certain minimum of rationality in this respect really modern government was impossible; and until the influence of the French Revolution began to be felt society over most of Europe was left to itself and to its own very slow rate of development. In the same way a society in which (as in most European states) a noble, a merchant, a peasant, and a priest had each a different legal personality with different rights and obligations, could not develop a modern legal system. Nor could a society in which guild and other corporate privileges were still so important easily produce efficient industries. With some exceptions, notably in France, the major rulers and governments of Europe during the eighteenth century achieved in these respects as much as could reasonably be demanded of them. Hardly any succeeded in breaking the bonds which circumstances imposed on them. This could be achieved only by revolution—either the revolution from above which Peter the Great partially carried out in Russia and which Joseph II unsuccessfully attempted in the Habsburg lands, or the more fundamental, dynamic, and self-sustaining revolution from below which France was to see from 1789 onwards.

**5**

# Intellectual and Artistic Life

IT IS ABOVE ALL in the flow of ideas and the growth of intellectual life that rapid development can be seen in eighteenth-
century Europe. In the intellectual world alone was there
relatively rapid mutation and adaptation to new knowledge and
new circumstances. And this intellectual change, like the slower
ones in society and economic life, accelerated from the 1750s
or 1760s.

The most obviously growing element in eighteenth-century
intellectual life was the physical sciences and the ideas and
assumptions associated with them. Europe during this period
produced no scientist of the epoch-making stature of Newton
or Galileo. Rather than making fundamental new discoveries
of the most far-reaching kind, it exploited and increased the
capital of scientific ideas and knowledge built up for it by the
giants of the preceding century, refining, elaborating, and
popularizing their ideas. Now for the first time some knowledge
of their discoveries and what they implied began to be widespread among the educated classes of Europe. Popular interest
in the physical sciences was growing rapidly. It has been
calculated that in the period 1750–89 not far short of 900
scientific periodicals were founded (many of them were of
course very short-lived) as against a mere 35 in the period
1665–99. Essentially literary journals, moreover, often printed
articles of scientific or technological interest—a sign that a
class of true specialists in the sciences was only beginning to
emerge and that an interest in them could still be thought of as

part of the intellectual equipment of the ordinary educated man. As early as 1693 the great English philosopher John Locke had said that a gentleman must 'look into' natural philosophy 'to fit himself for conversation'. There were even attempts to use scientific and quantitative methods in the solution of social problems; thus for example the Italian writer Tommaso Ceva in his *De Re Numeraria* (1711) tried for the first time to treat monetary problems mathematically, and a number of scholars, by applying the same methods to the problems of life expectancy, founded the science of demography. All over Europe by the middle of the century it was fashionable to perform scientific experiments and to attend the courses of public lectures on elementary science which were becoming increasingly common. The success of popular scientific works such as the Abbé Pluche's *Spectacle de la nature* (1732) and Joseph Priestley's *History and Present State of Electricity* (1767) was another proof of this growing interest. It was, of course, in the main a dilettante and shallow-rooted interest; already some branches of science were becoming too complex, and above all too mathematical in their language, to be easily comprehensible by the layman. But it was a striking new phenomenon, one of which there had been little sign during the seventeenth century.

Eighteenth-century scientific activity had serious limitations. In physics, astronomy, and mathematics, with the vast achievements of earlier generations to build on, much was accomplished. A line of great scholars, largely French—Maupertuis, d'Alembert, Lagrange, Laplace—developed and applied the ideas of Newton and assured their eventual acceptance throughout Europe. The beautiful symmetry and essential simplicity of Newtonian physics had important indirect results. It bred, even in those incapable of following its refinements or its mathematical expression, a new confidence in man's ability to understand and control his own environment, a new faith in the power of reason to penetrate the secrets of the universe. It also encouraged a marked bias towards deductive reasoning from relatively simple first principles as the most effective means of attacking any problem. This attitude tended more and more, as the century progressed, to influence the thinking of the educated on social, political, and religious questions. In other branches of science, however, progress was much slower and more difficult. Chemistry, handicapped by a remarkable slowness to adopt strict quantitative methods, made no fundamental advance until the work in the 1770s and 1780s of Priestley and Lavoisier on respiration, which led to the discovery of oxygen and the first real understanding of the process of combustion. Not until Lavoisier and Guyton de Morveau published their *Méthode de nomenclature chimique* in 1787 did chemists begin to have even the essential tool of a rational and generally agreed system of terminology. The lag in the development of the biological sciences was even more striking. They were far more resistant than physics or astronomy to the use of mathematical methods. In them far-reaching discoveries were much more difficult to make, unifying principles harder to establish. Elaborate systems of classification were worked out for plants by the Frenchman, Tournefort, at the beginning of the century and later by the Swede, Linnaeus, while the great French scholar, Buffon, attempted to do the same for animals; but the intellectual impact of all this was much less than that of Newton's work. The great prestige of the mathematics-based sciences meant that there was a tendency to dismiss biology, zoology, and even botany as unsuited to the sort of quantitative treatment which had yielded such wonderful results in physics, astronomy, or dynamics. It is significant that one of the few scientists of the period who openly distrusted the fashionable mathematical approach to scientific problems was Buffon, a zoologist.

Moreover eighteenth-century science was weakened and its scope restricted by the fact that it was very largely divorced from technology and everyday life. In medicine, now the most important of the applied sciences, this gap was very striking indeed. Harvey's discovery of the circulation of the blood, published as early as 1628, had completely exploded all the assumptions on which the very widespread practice of bloodletting as a cure for disease was based. Yet this remained a basic medical technique throughout the eighteenth century and was still very widely used as late as 1850. On the other hand vaccination against smallpox, which was becoming widespread in the later decades of the century, long before it was described by Edward Jenner in 1798, cut across all accepted medical theories; it was not until the second half of the following century that its workings were understood. This gap between scientific theory and professional or technological practice is seen repeatedly in the history of the period, notably in the fact that few of the great inventions upon which the Industrial Revolution in Britain was largely based owed anything to science and that many of them were the work of poorly educated men. (The important exception is the steam-engine, the development of which was considerably influenced by that of scientific knowledge and which was evolved in a scientific atmosphere.)

Upon political ideas the influence of the physical sciences was considerable though indirect. Many writers, especially during the second half of the century, tended to assume much too easily that the political and social world could be understood in the same way and by the same processes as the physical one. The movement of matter in space was now known, or thought to be known, to be governed by relatively simple general rules. Similar rules, it was too easily taken for granted, must govern human behaviour. Knowledge of them would give man the power to control the society in which he lived, to rebuild it on a more rational plan, to make it more just and efficient. He would thus ensure for himself the happiness which in 'enlightened' circles was more and more regarded as a right, and not as a fortunate and transient abnormality in an incomprehensible and generally painful world. This current of thought can be seen most clearly, though in varying forms, in France during the middle and later decades of the century in the works of such writers as d'Alembert, Helvétius, and d'Holbach. It underlay many though by no means all of the articles in the famous *Encyclopédie raisonnée des sciences et des arts*, inspired by Denis Diderot, which began publication in 1751. It was profoundly optimistic, not so much about human nature as about what could be done for and by imperfect human beings through the march of reason, expressed in the progress of science and the rational reconstruction of society.

The weaknesses of this attitude are easy to see from the perspective of two centuries later. It was generalized and intellectually absolutist; it ignored the extent to which societies and their needs and aptitudes differed in different parts of the world and at different times. Many of the thinkers of the Enlightenment, the great movement of liberal and often iconoclastic ideas which swept across Europe in the middle decades of the century, believed far too easily in the existence of fundamental principles, valid for all times and places and inherent in all human societies as gravitational attraction was in matter. It was a profoundly unhistorical attitude. The eighteenth century produced great historians such as the Englishman, Gibbon (1737–94), the Italian, Giannone (1676–1748), and the German, Schlözer (1735–1809), and one great philosopher of history, the Italian, Vico (1668–1744). But it was in general an unhistorical age, like all others before the nineteenth century; it lacked the imaginative understanding of the past which is the hallmark of the highest type of historian. It is rare during this period to find any systematic effort to explain social or political phenomena in terms of their growth through time. The Middle Ages in particular were usually regarded with contempt (except by a small minority of scholars such as the German, Justus Möser), though little effort was made to study them seriously or to discover why this 'incomprehensible aberration of the human mind', as Kant called them, had lasted so long. This lack of historical sense deprived much of the political and social thought of the eighteenth century of an important dimension. In particular it does a good deal to explain the lack of interest in institutions, as opposed to general ideas, which marks much of it. Radical thought on social problems was seldom based upon a real examination of political and economic mechanisms, as so much of that of the nineteenth century at least purported to be, but rather (as in the works of Morellet, Mably, Brissot de Warville, and for that matter Rousseau himself) upon essentially inductive views of an ideal social order. Socialist ideas (for example a denial that property was a natural right as Locke had argued) were fairly widespread before 1789, at least in France, but they were vague and insecurely based. Finally, much eighteenth-century thinking was based on an over-simplified and unimaginative view of human psychology derived ultimately from the English philosopher Locke and popularized by his many followers, notably by Condillac in France and Hartley in England. This stressed the physical senses and data acquired through them as the only valid sources of knowledge, and the acquisition of knowledge and the use of reason as the key to happiness.

The account of the social and political thought of this period given in the preceding paragraphs is, of course, one-sided and incomplete. The greatest figures in the intellectual life of the eighteenth century were not deceived into accepting the unproved assumptions and excessive optimism which characterized many of their followers. Neither Hume nor Kant, the two greatest philosophers of the century, shared the widespread 'enlightened' belief in the almost boundless powers of human reason. Voltaire (1694-1778) was the greatest and most tireless of all publicists of the Enlightenment; it is significant that he published, in 1738, the most influential though not the best popularization of Newton's scientific ideas. But he had no systematic political beliefs of his own and only limited interest in politics as such. His hatred of intolerance and obscurantism (at least when they were religious in origin) was genuine and constructive; but during the later decades of his long life his view of human nature and of the possibility of indefinite human progress became steadily more cynical. In its underlying pessimism and quietism his best-known work, the novel *Candide* (1759), has much in common with the *Rasselas* of Samuel Johnson published in the same year (as Johnson himself pointed out), though the one was the work of an anti-clerical *philosophe* and the other of a profound conservative. Nor was thinking at the highest level on social and political problems always contemptuous of history. A few serious efforts were made to explain social and political phenomena in historical and developmental terms, notably in the *Scienza Nuova* (1726) of Vico (which was completely neglected by his contemporaries) and the *Origines Iuris Civilis* (1713) of his fellow-Italian, Gravina. From a different point of view the German, J. G. Herder, stressed, against the universalism and cosmopolitanism which dominated educated Europe, the fundamental division of mankind into a great number of different groups and cultures, each with its own ideas and values.

Above all the two greatest political thinkers of the period, Montesquieu (1689–1755) and Rousseau (1712–78), do not fit into the simplified picture of the Enlightenment which has been painted above. Of all writers on social and political problems in modern history Montesquieu was one of the most fertile in ideas and one of the widest in intellectual scope; in these respects he is comparable with Aristotle himself. His importance stems above all from his interest in facts and his respect for them. He was one of the few really major political thinkers of the age who were profoundly interested in the practical problems of government. Almost alone among them he realized that good government, especially in large and complex states, was difficult to achieve and would not arise from the more or less mechanical application of a few general principles evolved *a priori*. It is significant that he was the only great writer on politics of the eighteenth century whose works were widely approved of by rulers and their ministers. His greatest book, *De l'esprit des lois* (1748), was being quoted as an authority in the Parlement of Paris only a year after it was published; the King of Sardinia ordered his son to read it, and in the Habsburg dominions the imperial librarian encouraged its diffusion. He did not exaggerate, as so many of his contemporaries did, the powers of rulers and governments or their ability to reform society from above. His influence therefore helped to counteract the danger, implicit in some though by no means all of the writings of Voltaire, that the Enlightenment might degenerate politically into a mere apologia for enlightened despotism. Some of Montesquieu's ideas, notably his belief in the power of climate to determine human psychology and hence the character of political institutions, were as mechanistic as those of any of his contemporaries. Others were highly schematic and *a priori*; notably his assumption that each form of rule has its own dominant principle—virtue in a republic, honour in a monarchy, fear in a tyranny. His use of certain key concepts—Nature and Law, for example—was as ambiguous as that of most other writers of the period. But it is his efforts to arrange great numbers of facts in meaningful patterns, seen above all in the *Esprit des lois* and to a lesser extent in his *Considérations sur les causes de la grandeur des Romains et de leur décadence* (1734) which makes him a writer of the highest distinction. He was not an historian; but he can be regarded, at least in a general sense, as one of the founders of sociology. This in itself gives him a relevance to present-day problems which most of his contemporaries do not possess.

If Montesquieu was from many points of view the most modern of the great political thinkers of the century, Jean-Jacques Rousseau was the most dynamic and the most revolutionary in his influence. Like so many of those who contributed to the development of eighteenth-century political thought—Voltaire, or Diderot, or even Montesquieu—Rousseau was not simply or even primarily a writer on politics. His novel, *La Nouvelle Héloise* (1761), his *Émile* (1762), one of the most visionary and influential works on education ever written, his self-revelation in his *Confessions* (1782), are from many points of view as important as his *Discours sur l'origine et les fondements de l'inégalité parmi les hommes* (1754) or his more widely read *Du contrat social* (1762). More than any other important writer on politics, he expressed ideas which were the outgrowth of his own tortuous and unhappy personality. He was not a systematic thinker. The history and working of existing institutions had no interest for him. He was above all a visionary; from this stem his strengths and weaknesses. His writings can be seen as a continuous and frustrated quest for self-fulfilment and through it the happiness which for ever eluded him. What he sought was a society which would be simpler and above all more egalitarian than those of civilized Europe, one which would not expose him to the snubs and ridicule, real or fancied, which he had had to endure in the salons of Paris. Such a society he sought with a fervour which was essentially religious; indeed he smuggled into politics through the back door the religious element which every other major thinker of the century sought, to one extent or another, to exclude. He himself admitted that his ideas were practicable, if at all, only in small and largely self-sufficient societies such as his native city-state of Geneva; his thinking was deeply influenced by memories of his Genevan upbringing. His only effort at constitution-making for a large state, the scheme for the reform of the Polish government which he drew up in 1771, was remarkably conservative in content. His most important innovation in the field of political ideas was probably the concept of the general will (*volonté générale*) which figures largely in his *Contrat social*. This was above all an effort to reconcile the selfishness of the individual, which was implicit in the psychology of Locke and admitted as a fact by all the thinkers of the Enlightenment, with the general good and the interests of society as a whole. To this central problem Adam Smith in his *Wealth of Nations* (1776) and Jeremy Bentham in his *Introduction to the Principles of Morals and Legislation* (1789) were later to propose other and very different answers. Rousseau attempted to solve the problem by assuming the existence in every society of a general will which expressed the highest aspirations of that society and the true desires of each member of it. How this general will was to be recognized he never made clear; but he insisted that it was different from and superior to the will of a mere numerical majority. Above all, local and sectional interests of all kinds, which might intervene between the government and its subjects and thus impede the expression of the general will, must be swept away. The immediate effect of Rousseau's political ideas was not great. But his radical utopianism, the aspiration which he expressed towards a perfect, egalitarian, and highly intolerant society, could have very dangerous implications, as the Jacobin dictatorship of 1793–4 in France was to show.

Upon religious belief the effect of scientific discovery in the eighteenth century was considerable; but it is an anachronism to speak of a conflict between science and religion in this period. As a result of Newton's discoveries, the physical universe seemed to mirror more clearly than ever before the power and perfection of God. In Britain and to a lesser extent in France scientists were normally, in some sense at least, religious believers. Already the study of fossils was beginning to show that the Biblical account of the history of the world was untenable; but as yet this had scarcely begun to shake the general faith in the reconcilability of science with religious orthodoxy. The damaging attacks to which traditional forms of religion were now being subjected came from other sources than the physical sciences.

The most important of these was the development of textual and historical criticism of the Bible, or at least of the Old Testament. This criticism stressed the internal inconsistencies of the Bible as an historical narrative and thus increasingly undermined the idea of Biblical infallibility. The seriousness of such attacks can be seen in the strength of the reaction they drew from the faithful; the most famous work of this kind, Richard Simon's *Histoire critique du vieux testament* (1678), provoked over forty replies in the generation which followed. Moreover growing knowledge of non-European peoples, above all of the Chinese (see p. 142), threw increasing doubt upon the traditional assumption that Christian belief was the only secure basis of virtuous conduct. If a Confucian, a Brahmin, even a savage in the wilds of North America, could behave as morally in everyday life as a Christian European, was it not possible that they stood in the same relation as he to God? Were truth and salvation perhaps after all not the monopoly of any church or any system of dogma? Knowledge of the outside world and the comparisons it made possible thus fostered in Europe a more tolerant and open-minded attitude in matters of religion. It was therefore a major source of the idea of 'natural religion' and of the deism which attracted so many members of the educated classes (Voltaire is the outstanding example) in the more advanced parts of the continent. Belief in natural religion also owed much to the development of physics and astronomy. Their vast successes, the new picture of the universe which they provided, weakened the traditional view of God as a jealous if loving Father preoccupied with the doings of his creation, Man. He was now seen rather as the source of the symmetry and regularity which dominated the universe, as a cosmic watchmaker supervising the workings of the machine which he had constructed. He now seemed more than ever before remote from human cares and joys. All men, it was argued, possessed certain innate religious ideas—the knowledge that God existed, that virtue would be rewarded and vice punished in some future life, and that there were certain fundamental laws which man must obey in his relations with his fellows. Obedience to these ideas and reverence for the God who continually manifested himself through the workings of the physical universe were all that was necessary for correct belief and conduct and therefore for salva-tion. Religious ceremonial, liturgical complexities, the useless and even destructive sophistications of academic theology, were mere corruptions of the true religion of nature. Only the in-tolerance and self-interest of clerics and the ignorance and submissiveness of the ordinary man explained their continued existence. The workaday virtues and the morality of the plain man, not mysticism or dogma, were the real core of religion. Anything which tended to complicate and obscure its essential simplicities, and thus to divide men from one another by generating religious dissension, must be resisted.

This attitude found favour among laymen disenchanted with traditional religious attitudes; it also affected thinking within the established churches. It powerfully influenced the Anglican church and does something to explain the growth during this period of Unitarianism as a small but intellectually important communion distinct from the Church of England. It had great influence within the Lutheran churches of Germany and Scandinavia, notably in Prussia, where the teaching of theology in the universities, above all at Halle, was strongly rationalist. Such a climate of opinion was obviously favourable to the development of religious toleration; and the century, especially its later decades, saw a steady movement in this direction. In France Protestants, who in 1703 had been goaded by persecu-tion into revolt in the Cevennes area, largely recovered their lost civil rights in 1787. In Britain the legal disabilities imposed on Catholics began slowly to crumble from 1778 onwards. In the Habsburg hereditary lands non-Catholics were granted freedom of religion in 1781. In many parts of Europe, most notably in Prussia and the Habsburg Empire, the legal and

social position of Jews greatly improved; already Locke and
Montesquieu had argued in favour of toleration for them and
by the 1780s a few radicals even in backward Poland were willing
to contemplate granting them equal political rights. Freemasonry, with its vague emphasis on reason and virtue and its
implicit hostility to many aspects of organized religion and the
established churches, spread rapidly over much of Europe, in
spite of papal condemnations in 1738 and 1751. Always relatively unimportant in the western states, it had become by the
1770s a significant ingredient in the intellectual life of Russia,
Poland, and some parts of Germany. The declining importance
of the antagonisms between Catholics and Protestants is also
seen in the fact that though they had still been a factor of some
significance in international affairs in the first half of the century
they lost this position by the 1760s or at latest the 1770s.

But it cannot be too strongly emphasized that the liberalizing
trends which have just been described were limited in their
scope. Everywhere they were confined to educated minorities.
Even in France, the centre of the Enlightenment, religious
toleration made headway with the greatest difficulty. There the
current of feeling known as Jansenism, which had emerged since
the middle of the seventeenth century, at first as an essentially
theological movement among scholars and from the later years
of Louis XIV as a more broadly-based and popular one,
suffered severe persecution. Theologically it laid heavy emphasis
on predestination as against free will. Politically most of its
importance came from its association with Gallicanism (the
traditional resistance of the church in France to papal claims
and control). On both counts it was hated by the orthodox and
the ultramontane. It received much support from the *parlements*, above all that of Paris, and from many French priests.
For nearly half a century it was a centre around which opposition to the old régime in France as well as to many aspects of
eighteenth-century Catholicism could rally. Its ideas won considerable support in other parts of Europe, notably in the
Netherlands and Italy. Yet by the 1760s it was clear that it had
been defeated in France and that it had little chance of victory
elsewhere. As far as the ordinary man was concerned, tolera-

tion, natural religion, and deism were everywhere strange and suspect.

At this social and educational level 'superstition was not imposed by the clergy from above; it welled up from the people below,' as a recent historian has put it. An obvious illustration of this point is the way in which popular resistance forced the immediate repeal of a bill, passed by large majorities in both houses of parliament in 1753, which would have allowed Jews to become naturalized British subjects without first being converted to Christianity and taking the sacraments according to the rites of the Church of England. Another is the fact that for a few days in 1780, during the Gordon Riots, London was completely at the mercy of a violent anti-Catholic mob. The torturing to death of an alleged witch near Angers in 1780 and the burning of another in Switzerland two years later, the almost universal horror felt for suicides and the indignities inflicted on their corpses, show how strong ancestral fears and intolerances still were. Over much of Catholic Europe indeed—in Spain, Portugal, Bavaria, and most of Italy—even the highest classes of society were still almost untouched by new ideas in religious matters. Thus in the 1740s the Jesuit confessor of Charles III of the Two Sicilies gave him a bag full of charms called 'tickets of the immaculate' which he was to wear continuously; if threatened by danger he was to swallow the charms. In Bavaria in 1777 the Elector Maximilian Joseph, on his deathbed, was forced to swallow a small crucifix in an effort to prolong his life. In Spain, where a man was burnt by the Inquisition as late as 1781, society from top to bottom was completely hostile to the idea of religious change. It was even more so in Portugal, where in the 1760s it was estimated that a tenth of the population was composed of monks, nuns, and priests.

None the less during the eighteenth century, above all from the 1760s onwards, many rulers and ministers curtailed the privileges of the Catholic church and still more the effective power of the Papacy in their dominions. Efforts were made (for example in Spain in 1737 and the early 1770s) to limit or abolish the right of sanctuary which allowed criminals to take refuge in churches from their pursuers. Monasteries and nunneries, often decayed, with few inmates and apparently contributing nothing to society, were a favourite target. In France a royal commission of 1768 suppressed a considerable number of religious houses and raised the minimum age at which religious vows could be taken. There the law of mortmain, intended to restrict legacies to the church, had already been drastically stiffened in 1749; and the idea of large-scale expropriation of church lands was gaining ground long before the Revolution. In Lombardy again, during the 1770s, the number of monasteries was halved and their income reduced by two-thirds. In Naples and Sicily under an anti-clerical minister, Bernardo Tanucci (1759–76), considerable efforts were made to reduce the burden on society constituted by the regular clergy, while in 1768 the Duke of Parma was excommunicated by Pope Clement XIII because of his attacks on the power of the church in the duchy. The Emperor Joseph II not merely introduced a high degree of religious toleration in his dominions but also suppressed over four hundred Catholic religious houses, as well as drastically limiting papal power in the Habsburg territories. The anti-papal 'Josephist' attitude expressed in his policies won wide popularity in Germany. It was to influence the relations of the Habsburgs with the Catholic church for the next half-century. Simultaneously Joseph's brother Leopold contemplated a complete overhaul of the system of church government in the Grand Duchy of Tuscany, though by 1787 the scheme had had to be abandoned as impracticable. By the last years of the century Baron Thugut, who had succeeded Kaunitz as chancellor in 1794, was contemplating the annexation by the Habsburgs of part of the Papal State.

The most striking demonstration of papal weakness and of the hostility of the secular powers of Catholic Europe to many aspects of the church as it then existed came with the suppression of the Jesuits. The Society of Jesus had always been intensely disliked by a great many Catholics. Its wealth and political influence, and also the real intellectual distinction of many of its members, aroused the envy of other orders. Its extreme papalism made it increasingly resented by monarchs and governments. In the third quarter of the century the hostility which had been accumulating for two hundred years burst forth dramatically. In 1759 the Jesuits were expelled from Portugal. In 1764 they were driven from France; in 1767 from Spain, the Two Sicilies, and Parma. In 1773 Pope Clement XIV, under heavy pressure from the French and Spanish governments, abolished the society by the brief *Dominus ac Redemptor Noster*. The greatest bastion of the spirit of the Counter-Reformation had been destroyed, and by the institution which it had done so much to preserve and strengthen. The crushing of the Society, which was often carried out with considerable and unnecessary brutality by the governments concerned, was an unmistakable indication of the growing refusal of the Catholic princes to tolerate any longer clerical rights which were inconvenient to them or religious institutions which seemed to threaten their power. Only the French Revolution and its aftermath, by making the church appear as the greatest bastion of the social and political *status quo*, could weaken and eventually reverse this attitude.

But none of this reflected any hostility on the part of Catholic rulers to the religious beliefs of their subjects or to Catholic dogma. Often indeed they were supported in their hostility to the papacy by the church hierarchy within their dominions. If various aspects of Catholicism were disliked by the secular rulers of Europe in the eighteenth century it was for political or economic, not philosophical or doctrinal reasons. If they came into conflict with the church, it was because of specific things it did or failed to do. They did not, like a small number of radical *philosophes*, object to its very existence. The violent and systematic anti-clericalism of Voltaire, for all the brilliance of its expression and the response it aroused among the educated classes over much of Europe, reflected the attitude of only a small segment of society. The eighteenth century was in a very real sense an age of reason, if by reason we mean hostility to traditional dogmas; but the effective scope of this reason was limited to certain social groups, certain geographical areas, and certain subjects. In religion, therefore, more than in politics or economic life, reason coexisted with a mass of traditional beliefs and assumptions, deeply-rooted and as yet largely beyond the reach of rational argument. Scarcely anywhere in Europe had the ordinary man ideas of his own on political or economic questions. Everywhere he had religious beliefs and emotions.

The dissemination of new ideas, scientific, political, or religious, owed little to the universities. This was not a great period in the history of university education. A few universities indeed made real contributions to the intellectual life of the age. The medical school of Leyden in the first half of the century and those of Edinburgh and Vienna in its later decades; the importance of Glasgow in the teaching of many of the physical sciences; the historical research and writing associated with Edinburgh and Göttingen—all these kept alive the idea of universities as centres of discovery and new ideas. But they shone out against the background of a system of higher education generally dominated by conservatism, timidity, and adherence to routine. The intellectual achievements of eighteenth-century France owed nothing to the country's universities and were in some ways even impeded by them. The same is broadly true of England, Italy, and Scandinavia. One of the most striking negative facts about the great revolutionary decade which began in 1789 is the almost completely negligible part played in it by the universities and their students and teachers; not until the last years of the Napoleonic Empire did they begin to have a significant political role anywhere in Europe.

Nor did the learned societies and academies (some of which were already well-established at the beginning of this period and many others of which were created during it) generally play a very creative role in its intellectual life. Some, notably perhaps the Academy of Sciences founded in Russia in 1725 under the inspiration of Peter the Great, had real cultural significance for their own areas. In general, however, their role was of only secondary importance. The Royal Society in Britain, the Académie des Sciences in France, both with a history of achievement in the later seventeenth century, lapsed into relative inertia during this period. Moreover the literary societies, which were numerous in most of western Europe, tended to be highly conservative and even obscurantist in their attitude, so that the papers read to them were far too often merely empty displays of learning divorced from contemporary problems. The insistence of one of the most famous, the Accademia della Crusca in Florence, that the only suitable medium of literary expression for its members was the Tuscan evolved in the fourteenth century, and that all later 'variety and barbarity' should be avoided, is an extreme but not very unfair illustration of the attitude of many of them.

The diffusion of ideas in eighteenth-century Europe was able to achieve hitherto unheard-of speed and effectiveness above all because of the growth of the press. Official censorship of the printed word, though still in operation in the more backward parts of Europe, was now less stringent than ever before in many of the relatively developed states. In Britain and the Dutch Republic restrictions on the free publication of books were now very slight. Even in France censorship, severe in theory (in 1785 there were 179 royal censors of books), was often very ineffective in practice. In Prussia an effort made in 1789 to revive and strengthen old censorship regulations had little practical result. In every European state the number of books published increased greatly during the eighteenth century; and in its second half the increase sometimes became very rapid indeed. The size of the catalogues of the annual Leipzig book fair, by far the most important of its kind in Europe, more than trebled in the two decades after 1770. To take an extreme example, in Russia, which at the beginning of the century had possessed only one printing-press, at least twenty-two were set up in the period 1783-96. Three hundred and sixty-six titles were published there in 1790 as compared with a mere thirty in 1760; and in 1768 there appeared the first attempt by a Russian author at a serious discussion of contemporary west European political theories. Above all, the later decades of the century saw a great growth in the publication of periodicals and the establishment of newspapers as an integral part of European life. The increasing number of scientific periodicals has already been mentioned (see p. 108) and a similar, though less rapid, growth can be seen in the popularity and influence of other forms of periodical publication. The first political monthly had been founded at The Hague in 1686, and in Britain the success of the *Spectator* (1711–14), perhaps the most famous of eighteenth-century literary periodicals, and of more general ones such as the *Gentleman's Magazine* (founded in 1731), and the *Scots Magazine* (founded in 1739), was a striking demonstration of the possibilities of the new form. The *Spectator* in particular was widely imitated and had real influence on the development of literary taste in many parts of Europe. From the 1740s onwards the appeal of periodicals was being increased by the use of engravings to illustrate them; by the 1780s colour engravings were possible.

Newspapers developed much more slowly than literary or scientific periodicals. Here too Britain was a pioneer; the first English daily paper appeared in 1702 and by 1724 three were being published in London. Elsewhere in Europe things moved more slowly in this respect. France had no daily paper until 1777 and the growth of the French newspaper press became marked only in the years immediately before the revolution, though it then developed rapidly. In Germany also it was not until later in the century that newspapers became an important and relatively independent influence. Nevertheless here too there was marked advance. Only seven mainly political periodicals were published in the German states during the 1770s; by the 1790s there were twenty-four. In areas such as Russia, Spain, Portugal, and most of Italy newspapers and periodicals were still in their infancy when the revolution began in France.

All this mass of printed matter did more than anything else to diffuse, often of course in a diluted and oversimplified form, the ideas of the age on intellectual, political, and social questions. The increasing production and growing accessibility of books, periodicals, and newspapers meant that by the last years of the period there was evolving, at least in a few of the wealthier and better-educated parts of Europe—the Netherlands, Britain, France, some of the German states—a public opinion of something like a modern kind. Preaching, Bible-reading, and clerical influences on education had ensured that the ordinary man over most of western and central Europe had always had some contact with religious ideas and controversies.

Now for the first time in history relatively sophisticated ideas on political and social problems might become equally accessible to him. The dangers of this were only too visible to contemporaries. They explain the anxiety of governments, even in Britain, to retain influence over, if not outright control of, the press. But this great expansion of the audience for writing on political and social problems could scarcely now be halted, far less reversed. In the Europe of the later eighteenth century it was one of the most important premonitions of the new age in which the old régime was soon to be dissolved.

In art, literature, and music the eighteenth century was a richly productive age, though it hardly equalled, except in music, those which had given rise to Michelangelo and Shakespeare. Its variety and fecundity, however, make impossible a brief description of its achievements in these fields without a good deal of oversimplification; and the paragraphs which follow are a very bare and inevitably incomplete summary of its achievements.

In literature and the visual arts it is possible to draw, in the most general terms, a number of contrasts between the first and second halves of the century. The art and literature of its first half, at least on what contemporaries thought of as their highest levels, tended to be solemn, formal, often impersonal, consciously uplifting and didactic. The artist, and above all the writer, was to concern himself with the permanent, universal, and generalized aspects of his subject rather than with the more individual, transitory, and personal ones. In literary theory, which was now being produced in hitherto unparalleled quantities, this attitude can be seen in the general assumption that the epic and the ode were the highest forms, not merely of poetry but of literature in general. This meant the relegation of all prose writing, and above all of the novel, which now seems the most interesting and important literary form of the period, to a position of inferiority. In art and architecture a recognizably similar mode of feeling can be seen in the baroque styles which, surviving from the previous century, also aimed at uplifting and impressing the observer and were also marked, at their best, by a somewhat self-conscious nobility and an impressive gravity, and at their worst by a wearisome heaviness and rigidity. Even amongst professional critics and writers on aesthetics these essentially conservative and aristrocratic attitudes did not go unchallenged during the first half of the century. It was always clear to at least some of them that genius was quite different from taste (Diderot's early critical writings illustrate this point well) and that imagination and personal emotions were at least as much the foundation of great painting, architecture, and writing as adherence to academic rules. Moreover in England and France Defoe, Prévost, and later Richardson and Fielding were producing novels which escaped altogether from the restrictions which taste and tradition imposed upon the more elevated forms of literature. In painting a similar escape from correctness to realism can be seen in the work of Hogarth in England and Chardin in France; and Watteau, the greatest painter of the early eighteenth century, developed a highly personal style which may have owed something to Chinese influences.

By the middle decades of the century both literature and art were feeling more and more the impact of new forces. Writers were now being influenced more than ever before by an interest in the past, by the belief that the poetry produced by a people is an expression of its history and character, by an interest in the literature of the Middle Ages, hitherto totally neglected, and in that of remote and primitive peoples. The historicism and exoticism which were now becoming so influential can be seen in the assembly of the first great collections of folk-songs, made by Bishop Percy in England (1756) and by Herder in Germany; in the first stirrings of interest in Dante (though a widespread understanding of his greatness as a poet was achieved only in the nineteenth century) and in the extraordinary though temporary popularity of James Macpherson's *Works of Ossian* (1765), a largely spurious collection of allegedly ancient Celtic poems. In art the general trend of development was in some ways similar. The excavation of Pompeii and Herculaneum from the 1740s onwards helped to stimulate a revival of interest in classical architecture, statuary, and art of all kinds. This was

fed during the next generation by a stream of remarkable published descriptions, accurate and copiously illustrated by draw-
ings and plans, of the great buildings of classical antiquity,
above all those of Greece and the eastern Mediterranean. The
neo-classical style which this helped to evolve was often remarkably elegant. Originated, as far as architecture and decoration
were concerned, largely by the Adam brothers in Great Britain
from the end of the 1750s, it offered a striking contrast to the
rococo decorative styles of the middle decades of the century,
with their frequent complexity and their dislike of symmetry
and geometric patterns. Like literature, art and architecture
were becoming more historically minded than ever before. There
were even signs of a dawning interest in Gothic architecture
(the French architect Soufflot produced a remarkably favourable discussion of it as early as 1741 in his *Parallèle des églises
gothiques avec les églises modernes*), though until the end of the
century it remained a very minor element in the artistic life
of Europe.

Literature and the arts were now being influenced also by a
growing cult of sensibility, by an increasing and excessive
emphasis on personal emotion as the essential subject-matter of
the painter and above all of the writer. While the first half of
the century had reasoned about literature and art the second
half increasingly wished to feel, rather than fully understand,
their impact, and to be presented with uplifting and purifying
models of virtue, high-minded emotion, and undeserved suffering. The writing and painting produced in these years, like
those of the earlier decades of the century, were largely didactic;
but the lessons they taught were essentially those of feeling.
They were more emotional, more focused on the individual,
more feminine, in a word more modern, than the aristocratic
and masculine assumptions of the previous generation. In
literature this stress on sensibility and the emotions achieved
its first great success with Richardson's *Pamela* (1740) and rose
to a peak with Goethe's *Sorrows of Werther* (1774) and the
rather ridiculous *Paul et Virginie* of Bernardin de St. Pierre
(1789). In painting, where it was never so widespread nor
carried to such lengths, it is perhaps best seen in the sentimental

and moralistic scenes of family life of the French artist Greuze.

The contrast which has been drawn in the preceding paragraphs, between the essentially seventeenth-century styles and modes of thought of the early part of this period and the historicism, neo-classicism, primitivism, and sensibility of its middle and later decades is of course a very rough one. Perhaps it hides as much as it reveals and falsifies as much as it explains. Certainly it would be very misleading to imply that there was any clear progression which can be easily mapped in time and space from one phase, one set of cultural assumptions, to another. Thus the idea, so generally accepted in the early eighteenth century, that the task of literature and the arts was to reflect only an idealized, generalized, and refined version of Nature, was emphatically restated by Sir Joshua Reynolds in the speeches which he delivered at the annual banquet of the Royal Academy from 1769 onwards. In the same way the stress on sensibility, on grief, tears, religious emotionalism, and general sentimentality, which became increasingly dominant in literature from the 1750s or 1760s, can be seen in a good deal of English poetry a generation earlier. In France it had begun to be visible, in a different and more intellectualized form, as early as 1719 in one of the most important critical works of the century, the *Reflexions critiques sur la poésie et sur la peinture* of the Abbé du Bos. The literary and artistic life of Europe in the eighteenth century was more complex than ever before. Its slow rediscovery of history and the fact that for the first time it was being influenced to some extent by non-European models meant that it had now at its disposal an unprecedentedly wide range of styles. The impossibility of forcing it into any conceptual strait jacket therefore becomes steadily greater as the century progresses. Clearly, however, by the middle of the century these aspects of European life were becoming modern in a way hitherto unknown. The rise in the importance of the novel and the undermining of the status of the poet which this involved; the cult of sensibility, which provided much of the foundation for the nineteenth-century one of the artist as a rebel against society; the growing popularity of genre painting, which was to reach its full height in the following century; the

growing distrust of rigid artistic or literary rules—all these
point to the future.

It is not easy to establish any convincing connexion between the
development of literature and the visual arts on the one hand
and music on the other. Some parallels and points of contrast
can nevertheless be seen. The Italian operas which so dominated
European music in the first half of the century, with their plots
drawn from history and classical mythology, their often elaborate and expensive stage-settings, and their ornate and technic-
ally difficult musical style, can perhaps be regarded as the
equivalent of the baroque in art and literature. Like it they
were the product of a society in which aristocratic values predominated, and were intended for the educated and well-born
rather than for popular consumption. Like it they expressed
real human emotions, but in a grave, stylized, and rather
impersonal way. In France above all there were obvious if
limited contacts between music and the wider world of ideas.
Rousseau was deeply interested in music, was himself the
author of two operas and fragments of an uncompleted third,
and in his *Lettre sur la musique française* (1753) of one of the
most important academic studies of the subject published during
this period. Voltaire was in the 1730s deeply involved in the
controversies between the great French composer Rameau and
his critics; and Rameau's *Traité de l'harmonie réduite à ses
principes naturels* (1722), the first major work ever written on
the theory of composition, may almost be regarded as an attempt
to do for music what Newton had done for physics. Throughout
the century, indeed, the idea of music as a science was becoming
stronger. In particular its relationship to mathematics was now
being systematically explored for the first time, notably by the
great Swiss mathematician Leonhard Euler.

This effort to establish equivalences between music and other
aspects of intellectual life can be pushed further. The reaction
against the styles and conventions of Italian *opera seria* which
was becoming marked by the middle of the century over most
of Europe, and the rise in the status of instrumental as against
vocal music which this involved, can be seen as the counterpart

of the movement in literature away from the conventions of the baroque, and the increased importance which this gave to prose, above all to the novel, as against poetry. In opera the increasing popularity of more realistic and demotic forms, the *opera buffa* in Italy, the ballad opera in England, the *Singspiel* in Austria, is a rough equivalent of the growing literary taste for realism and for a less sophisticated expression of the emotions. The great neo-classical operas of Gluck, such as *Orfeo ed Euridice* (1762) and *Alceste* (1767), which attempted to revive in musical form some of the spirit and outlook of Greek classical tragedy, have a clear affinity with such an expression of neo-classicism in art as the German critic Winckelmann's *Thoughts on the Imitation of Greek Works in Painting and Sculpture* (1755).

Both in music and literature these changes reflected changes in the social composition of the public which heard or read their products. The great significance of opera in European musical life during the earlier decades of the century was possible because as yet the public concert, nowadays the most important aspect of professional music-making, scarcely existed. (The first series of concerts open to the public was founded in Hamburg in 1722.) The opera-house, which was, except to some extent in Italy, the creation of princes and normally open to only the higher ranks of society, had therefore a degree of musical importance which it was never again to achieve. The taste for greater realism in opera and the rise in the status of instrumental music reflect on the other hand the slow emergence of a wider, largely middle-class, musical public. This was in turn made possible by the growth of the concert system and the development of the first significant printed musical criticism.

But it would be a great mistake to press too far these somewhat strained analogies between the development of music and that of other aspects of European life. The musical legacy left by the eighteenth century was richer than its literary one and far richer than that in the visual arts. The greatest creative figures in the music of the period—Bach (1685–1750), Handel (1685–1759), Haydn (1732–1809), Mozart (1756–91)—must be judged in their own terms. To apply to them the slipshod though unavoidable categories of baroque, rococo, neo-classical, or romantic is to belittle them and to convey a spurious impression of precision to the reader. Inevitably, all were in various ways moulded by their social and intellectual environment. Thus Bach (whose contemporary reputation did not match that which posterity has agreed to give him) drew inspiration from the quietist and conservative piety of Lutheran north Germany. Handel, a much more cosmopolitan figure, came from a somewhat similar environment but was deeply influenced by Italian music as Bach never was. Haydn, the first German composer to achieve a genuine international reputation, was affected by the Catholicism which pervaded so much of life and society in the Habsburg Empire; and Mozart, the most complex and unhappy of the four, had clear sympathies with some aspects of the Enlightenment, particularly perhaps with Freemasonry. None of them, however, was well educated or had any wide range of intellectual interests. It makes little sense to judge them in any but musical terms; and at least at its highest levels music, the most abstract and autonomous of the arts, is very difficult to dissect and categorize.

# 6
# Europe and the World

THROUGHOUT THE eighteenth century relations with the outside world played a steadily increasing part in the life of Europe.
This they did in two main ways. The first, and from most points
of view the more important, was through the steady growth of
trade between Europe and other continents. The colonial
empires of the period were to most Europeans essentially trading
concerns. This was less true of the great British and, above all,
Spanish colonies of settlement in America than of the more
fragile French and Dutch empires; but in general trade was the
most important force underlying overseas expansion in the
eighteenth century. Every imperial power attempted by complex legislation to confine trade with its own colonies to its
own ships and subjects. In every empire the ideal was that the
colonies should complement the economy of the mother country by sending her products, above all tropical products such as
sugar, tobacco, coffee, cotton, and indigo, which she could not
produce for herself. These might provide the basis for new
industries—sugar-refining, the manufacture of cotton textiles—
in the mother country; or they might be profitably re-exported
to those parts of the continent which had no colonies of their
own. The colonies should also provide a market for the manufactured goods of the mother country and, if necessary, a
receptacle for her surplus population. (Though in the eighteenth
century, when under- rather than over-population seemed to
economists the danger threatening most European states, this
last idea was relatively unimportant.) Restrictive colonial sys-

tems of this kind were not always intended merely as devices for the exploitation of the colonies. Underlying them was sometimes a genuine ideal of mutual help and support. If the colonies were allowed to export their products only to the mother country, these products were also normally given a monopoly there. This meant, for example, that the sugar of the British West Indian islands was able to command an artificially high price in the British market because of the exclusion from Britain of the cheaper sugar produced in the French islands. But very few people in Europe as yet thought of colonies as possessing rights equal to those of the European states. They and their inhabitants were clearly in a position of inferiority; in any conflict of interest they must give way to the needs and demands of the imperial power concerned.

The best-known and most intensively studied of these bodies of restrictive legislation is the British Navigation System. Originating in the Navigation Ordinance of 1651 it had become by the end of the seventeenth century a formidably complex mass of rules and enactments which confined colonial trade to British or colonial ships and attempted to sever all commercial contact between the British colonies and foreign states. In both France and Spain legislation governing colonial trade was in at least one sense even more limiting. In both, this trade was confined to certain parts of the country and even to certain towns. Thus in France a royal decree of 1717 allowed only thirteen specified ports to trade with the French colonies. (Nine others had been added to the list by the end of the Seven Years War.) In Spain during much of the century the American empire was still thought of as the possession of Castile alone rather than of the country as a whole. The monopoly of trade with it, hitherto enjoyed by the merchant oligarchy of Seville and Cadiz, was somewhat eroded by the formation with government support of new trading companies in northern Spain: the Caracas Company founded in 1728 was the most important of these. But it was not until 1765 that trade with America began to be opened to all Spanish ports; and this process was not complete until 1789. The confining of trade with India and south-east Asia to a number of privileged companies—the

French, Swedish, Danish, and above all Dutch and British East India Companies—showed in a different and more intense form the same monopolistic attitude.

These restrictive trade systems were not easy to enforce thoroughly; indeed it was almost impossible to make theory and practice coincide in great and rapidly evolving empires such as those of Britain and Spain. The Navigation System proved increasingly difficult to work in the North American colonies during the eighteenth century, above all in New England, where economic forces were driving Massachusetts, Connecticut, and other colonies into increasingly close relations with the French West Indies. Moreover the beginnings of industrial development in the British settlements and the growth of their strength and self-confidence were making them steadily less fitted for the subordinate position to which the System condemned them, and less willing to accept it. In Spanish America difficulties arose rather from the extreme weakness of Spanish industry and its complete inability to satisfy the colonial demand for manufactured goods. The inevitable result was that textiles, hardware, and other manufactures were smuggled into Spanish America by British and Dutch ships in great quantities, and sugar, tobacco, dyewoods, and bullion smuggled out to pay for them, so that the official trade regulations became more and more a farce. It was officially reported to Madrid, for example, that in the years 1706–21 not a single ship from Spain had entered the ports of Venezuela, while up to twenty Dutch ships traded regularly along the same coast. Partly because of these difficulties of enforcement, partly because of the slow growth of a new climate of opinion in commercial matters, there was a tendency towards liberalization of at least some branches of colonial trade from the 1760s onwards. This can be seen in the gradual admission of all Spanish ports to trade with America and also in the growth of a system of free ports in the British West Indies after 1766. But throughout the century the attitude of the imperial powers of Europe to their colonies and their trade with other continents remained essentially restrictive and exclusive.

This emphasis on trade as the main foundation of empire

meant that certain types of overseas expansion were regarded much more favourably than others. The West Indian islands were clearly, at least in the short run, the most profitable colonial possession of all. They produced commodities for which there was a rapidly growing demand in Europe and which could therefore provide, as they notably did in France, the basis for a profitable re-export business. Adam Smith described sugar, with reason, as more profitable than 'any other cultivation that is known either in Europe or America'. The insatiable West Indian demand for African slaves (the little British island of Barbados alone seems to have imported about 200,000 in the period 1712–68) was the foundation of European trade with West Africa. Some of the islands might be used as bases from which profitable smuggling into Spanish America could be carried on. Since most of them were now geared exclusively to the production of one staple crop, sugar, and had no industries whatever, they were exceptionally good markets for European manufactured goods. In 1738 a British pamphleteer argued that a planter in the West Indies, because of the imports he and his slaves consumed and the British shipping they employed, contributed to the national wealth twenty times as much as an Englishman who stayed at home. These factors explain the rapid growth of British and French trade with the West Indies during the century and the bitterness with which Britain and France contested control of these islands.

Trade with the British colonies of North America increased almost as fast. By the later 1720s their much greater white population had allowed them for the first time to surpass the West Indies as a market for British exports, and throughout the century their raw materials made a steadily growing contribution to British industry and re-exports. By 1771, admittedly a peak year in trade with America, just over half of all exports from Scotland consisted of American tobacco. This remarkable development of British and, to a lesser extent, French trade with the Western Hemisphere meant that throughout the century both powers were becoming less European in the pattern of their commerce. In the four-year period 1701–5 the American colonies (including the West Indies and Nova Scotia) took just under a tenth of all English exports and supplied rather less than a fifth of all English imports. In 1766–70 they took a little under a quarter of all British exports and supplied over a third of Britain's imports. Moreover this growth of Britain's transatlantic trade was interrupted only temporarily by the coming of American independence. In France a similar tendency can be seen in a less marked form. In 1715 about 13 per cent. of her trade was with America; by 1785 the proportion had more than doubled to 28 per cent., though most of the increase was concentrated in the two decades after 1763. Such a marked change in the geographical pattern of their commerce was bound to have political repercussions in both countries. In Britain it does much to explain the concentration on colonial and trade issues which is so noticeable in public discussion of foreign policy, and the hostility to large commitments or expenditures in Europe which flowed from it. In France it is one reason, though by no means the only one, for the tendency to turn away from Europe, to abandon old friendships with Poland and the Ottoman Empire in favour of commercial and maritime expansion, which becomes marked after the end of the Seven Years War.

By comparison European trade with Africa and the East was unimportant. In tropical Africa (the Barbary states of Morocco, Algiers, Tunis, and Tripoli were really part of the Mediterranean world) there was no permanent European settlement; and though the population of the Dutch colony at the Cape of Good Hope was growing, it was not in itself of much economic significance. Though the African market for European goods was expanding—British exports to Africa were valued at £130,000 in 1720 and £866,000 in 1775—it was still a very secondary one. It was not until 1765 that Britain first attempted to establish a colonial government there, with the creation of Senegambia; and the experiment collapsed in less than two decades. Except for slaves the continent produced nothing that Europeans wanted save small quantities of gold, aromatic gums, and ostrich feathers. The slave trade was certainly of great importance in the maritime economies of western Europe; and its results in Africa were perhaps not so completely negative

as is sometimes argued. But apart from this trade black Africa
meant almost nothing in the life of eighteenth-century Europe.
It remained largely unknown, partly because of the geographical
obstacles to travel in the interior (which have often been considerably exaggerated) and partly because native rulers in
coastal areas often strove to prevent their neighbours further
inland from trading with Europeans or obtaining arms from
them.

In Asia the position was different and more interesting.
Europe's trade with the East was far smaller than with the
transatlantic world. In the middle decades of the century the
British East India Company sent only about twenty ships to
India each year, whereas it was claimed that in the 1730s trade
with Jamaica alone employed 300 British merchantmen and
their crews. The Dutch Company for its part dispatched on
an average only twenty-nine ships annually to all its eastern
possessions in the first half of the century; and from the 1740s
onwards there was a perceptible fall in the efficiency with which
Dutch voyages to the East were conducted. This was reflected in
very heavy losses of seamen and meant that in the last fifty years
of the Company's existence (it collapsed in 1795) the number of
vessels engaged in trade with the East Indies tended to fall. By
comparison the trade of the relatively minor Dutch American
colony of Surinam employed an average of sixty to seventy
ships each year by the 1760s (though it is true that nearly all of
these were smaller than the vessels sent to the East).

If the eastern trade of Britain and the Dutch, the dominant
commercial powers of the area, was so limited, that of their com-
petitors was unlikely to flourish. The Danish Asiatic Company
set up in 1732 had some success in its trade with China; but in
its Indian trade it suffered constant losses, so that in 1772 its
monopoly was abolished and in 1777 the few trading factories it
had established were taken over by the Danish government. Its
Swedish counterpart traded on an equally limited scale and had
equally limited influence. The Habsburgs made several attempts
to develop an eastern trade from their Netherlands dominions,
but with little success. The Ostend Company founded in 1719
was crushed by British and Dutch jealousy; and an East India

Company set up in 1750 was a failure, as was the Imperial Trieste Company founded in 1775 (which in spite of its name was also based on Ostend). Even the French Compagnie des Indes Orientales always suffered from lack of capital and of effective government backing. In the struggles with its British rival in the 1740s and 1750s for political control of the Carnatic and parts of the Deccan, in south-eastern and southern India, it was decisively worsted. After vain efforts to escape from a hopeless financial position it became bankrupt and was dissolved in 1769; though it was revived in 1785, it had by then ceased to count seriously in Indian trade and politics.

The East, then, could never compare with America as a factor in European economic life. Sheer difficulty of access, the fact that Bombay was far harder to reach than Boston, or Canton than Charleston, in part accounted for this. But the main impediment to trade was the near-impossibility of finding European goods which the Indians and Chinese wished to buy in large quantities. It meant that oriental silk, tea, drugs, porcelain, and other goods had to be paid for largely by the export of gold and silver. Thus 93 per cent. by value of all the cargoes taken to Canton by the Danish Asiatic Company during the century, and 79 per cent. of those which went to India, consisted of bullion. Until the end of this period most economists regarded with the deepest suspicion a trade which involved such a loss of precious metals to pay for luxury and semi-luxury goods. Eastern trade, unlike that with America, was not in articles of mass consumption. Neither governments nor public opinion in western Europe regarded it with the favour they showed to transatlantic commerce.

It is true that from the 1760s onwards there were clear signs of growing British and, to some extent, French activity in the East. There was a rapid development of trade with Canton, the port to which all European commerce with China was confined by the Chinese government from 1757 onwards. In particular there was a striking increase in trade between British India and China, since Indian commodities were usually easier to sell in the Chinese market than British ones. New possibilities were not neglected. Warren Hastings, the greatest of all British proconsuls in India, was the first Englishman to grasp the potentialities of the Suez route as a line of communication between Europe and the East; in 1774 he sent an emissary to Tibet in the hope of gaining access overland to the great Chinese market; and in 1778-9 tried to open trade relations with the kingdom of Cochin-China in south-east Asia. There was also a revival of interest in the old dream of a north-west passage, a sea route which would unite the Atlantic and Pacific around the north of the American land mass. Of this the most important result was the discoveries made by Captain James Cook on his last and greatest voyage in 1776-9. Underlying all these developments was the consolidation and extension of British power in India. Clive's conquest of Bengal in the later 1750s was followed in 1764 by the defeat at Buxar of the Nawab of Oudh and the Great Moghul himself. Nine years later the Regulating Act of 1773 attempted to cope with the unprecedented problems created by the rise of a trading company to the position of a great territorial power.

On the French side a similar growth of interest in the East, sometimes mingled with hopes of revenge for the defeats France had suffered there, can be seen in various forms. It is visible in proposals of 1776 for a trading-station on Kilwa off the coast of East Africa; in much exploratory and scientific work in the Pacific; in a treaty of 1787 with Cochin-China; and above all in the growth in Paris of the idea that, when the Ottoman Empire collapsed as it soon must, Egypt might become a French possession, a greater tropical colony than any France already held. Even Spain showed an unaccustomed interest in eastern expansion by founding an unsuccessful Royal Philippine Company in 1785.

Yet the idea of a 'swing to the East' in the imperial and commercial interests of the west European powers during the generation after 1760 has probably been overstressed in recent writing. British trade with Asia certainly expanded; but this was part of a general commercial growth which embraced trade with America as well. There was no development of French trade with India and China at all comparable to the great boom in that with the West Indies which began soon after the peace of 1763. In both Britain and France the attention of statesmen and public opinion continued to be focused on America and the Caribbean, accessible areas where large numbers of white men had settled and created new societies. By comparison events in India or China seemed to the ordinary Englishman or Frenchman to take place in a different world, almost on a different planet.

The impact of the outside world upon Europe was not merely economic. There was also the influence, fluctuating, unevenly distributed, and often impossible to measure accurately, which knowledge of other parts of the world was now exerting upon European thought and culture. On the political level European thinking was obviously and directly affected by the American Revolution. The success of the thirteen colonies in throwing off British rule; their construction of a great new federation with almost unlimited possibilities of future expansion; their conscious and deliberate underlining of the fact that they represented a new type of society and a new outlook on life—all these aroused a warm response in many parts of western Europe. To opponents of the *status quo* in France and the Dutch Republic, and in Britain herself, the victory of the Americans seemed a hopeful augury, a sign that the forces of conservatism and privilege were not invincible. It showed that a more natural and efficient form of society and government, without privileged institutions, an established church, or a hereditary ruling class, could be achieved. It was only in the more intellectually and economically advanced parts of Europe that such feelings were widespread. In the Iberian peninsula, most of Italy, much of Germany, and all central and eastern Europe, there was little interest in the American Revolution or understanding of its implications. But throughout much of the Atlantic seaboard of the continent admiration for what the Americans had achieved was widespread, indeed often excessive. The American Revolution, wrote one observer, was 'a miracle of nationalism and patriotism . . . which has left the world overwhelmed with admiration'. This was a somewhat extreme but not very untypical expression of a widely-held point of view. For the first time European political thinking, and even action, were being deeply influenced by events in another continent. Even those who doubted whether the revolution across the Atlantic was legally or morally justified had no doubt that it was an event with vast implications for the future of the world. 'By and by,' wrote a German commentator in the early 1780s, 'America will rise, and as it climbs upwards Europe will sink . . . America will first weaken the economic and then the political power of European states, take away their possessions in the West Indies, and the new world will then become the conqueror of the old.' Few of his contemporaries would have gone as far as this; but the virtually unlimited potentialities of the new state across the Atlantic aroused widespread admiration and awe.

Yet this American influence was slow to develop—it hardly existed before the 1770s—and was confined to the sphere of political aspirations. In a strictly cultural sense America remained almost a nullity as far as eighteenth-century Europe was concerned. The influence of China, on the other hand, was surprisingly strong in the arts and in many aspects of European thought until late in the century. Already the age of Louis XIV had seen a growth of interest in China, fostered above all by the writings of Jesuit missionaries there. In 1687 there appeared in Paris the first attempt at a translation of Confucius; and throughout the following century selected letters and essays by Jesuits with experience of China appeared in sets which often ran to dozens of volumes. As early as 1739 the Royal Library in Paris possessed nearly 400 books in Chinese or Manchu, and its collection was growing rapidly. In 1777 the first large-scale history of the country written in a European language, by Father de Mailla, was published in Paris. The amount of information about China available to an educated European was therefore very substantial; but its quality did not match its quantity. The difficulties of the language, and those of assimilating a system of ideas in many ways totally alien to any current in Europe, created much misunderstanding. The same was true in the arts. During the seventeenth century there had been widespread admiration of Chinese pottery, furniture, and decorative styles; and in 1721 the German, Fischer von Erlach, made the first effort to provide a systematic account of Chinese architecture. Voltaire's *Orphelin de la Chine* (1755) was one of the most successful plays written during the eighteenth century; in 1762–8 Catherine II built a 'Chinese' palace at Oranienbaum; and in 1781 the ruler of Hesse-Kassel constructed a complete 'Chinese' village on the shores of the Wilhelmshöhe lake. But all this interest did not imply understanding. The vases and dishes imported in such quantities merely familiarized Europeans with the decorative styles then current in China. The ceramics of the T''ang and Sung dynasties, by far the greatest Chinese achievement in this field, remained totally unknown to them until the twentieth century. The passion for porcelain as a decorative material which inspired such achievements as the 'porcelain rooms', built in the 1750s and 1760s at Capodimonte and Aranjuez for the kings of Naples and Spain, was merely an aspect of rococo art in Europe. The 'Chinese' architecture of the eighteenth century was a curious hybrid, a tribute to the imagination and sometimes the taste of its creators but not to their knowledge of China. Though the styles of some artists, notably Watteau and Boucher in France, were probably affected by the Chinese paintings now available in Europe, this influence was neither deep nor widespread.

Yet with all their limitations cultural contacts with China had profound repercussions in Europe. Far more than those with any other part of the world they stimulated Europeans to re-examine their assumptions about the nature of history, of government, of religion, of man himself. Already in the seventeenth century the problem of reconciling Chinese chronology with that of the Bible had begun to exercise the devout; in the eighteenth century growing acceptance of the great antiquity of Chinese records led to an increasing readiness to see the Flood, which they did not mention, as a merely local event. Even Biblical criticism, still in its infancy, thus owed something during this period to Chinese influences. More potentially explosive in its immediate results was the fact that the Chinese had constructed a great civilization, and apparently reached a high level of personal morality, without the help of a revealed religion or of sacred books in the Judaeo-Christian or Moslem sense. Virtue and practical success could thus coexist with what looked suspiciously like atheism, a discovery which critics of established religious assumptions found increasingly congenial. Even at the end of the seventeenth century the French writer Pierre Bayle (1647–1706) had used China as a proof that morality, and therefore a stable society, could exist independently of religion, and had praised the religious tolerance which existed there as an example to be copied in Europe. This line of argument was not easy for orthodox Christians to refute; and it was one widely used by sceptics and deists until well into the second half of the eighteenth century, so that, as one writer has put it, 'Confucius became a sort of patron saint of the thinkers of the Enlightenment.'

On a more mundane level China also seemed to offer Europe an example of good government worthy of her imitation. European writers realized that she was a despotism. Indeed they tended greatly to exaggerate the effective powers of the emperor. But his rule seemed to many of them a 'legal despotism', one which accorded as far as possible with the laws of nature, and not the purely arbitrary 'oriental despotism' which Montesquieu so bitterly attacked in his *Esprit des lois*. China appeared a model of what might be achieved by an intelligent and public-spirited autocrat served by enlightened officials and unimpeded by an established church, a hereditary nobility, or entrenched privileged bodies. This attitude, which found its most famous expression in Voltaire's *Essai sur les moeurs* (1761–3), grossly idealized the realities of Chinese political life and often used the Chinese empire merely as a peg upon which to hang criticism of current abuses in Europe. Nevertheless in France at least it was very influential in the 1750s and 1760s. There many of the Physiocrats, notably Quesnay, whom his followers referred to as 'the European Confucius', were loud in their admiration of the government of China. In 1756, under their influence, Louis XV ceremonially ploughed with his own hands the first furrow in a field near Versailles. This was done in deliberate imitation of the ceremonial spring ploughing by the emperors of China and was perhaps the most curious of all illustrations of Chinese influence in eighteenth-century Europe.

Already, however, the attraction of Chinese models, artistic
or political, had begun to fade. In the arts Chinese influence,
never deep-rooted, was now being challenged by the growth of
new fashions and styles. In particular it was being replaced by
neo-classicism which was to become the most important artistic
influence in Europe in the last decades of the century, and by a
slowly-reviving interest in the Middle Ages which was to bear
fruit in neo-Gothic architecture and to become one of the main
components of Romanticism (see pp. 127–8). The view of China
as a model of good government had never been without critics;
and by the 1760s many of the most vociferous *philosophes*—
Helvétius, d'Holbach, Diderot—were generally unsympathetic
to it. Above all Rousseau, to whom Chinese civilization represented the artificiality and sterility which he wished to replace
with simplicity and naturalness, disliked everything Chinese.
The sinophil feeling which reached its peak in Europe, above
all in France, in the middle of the century, is a unique episode
in the history of ideas. But it was always artificial and insecurely
based; it could hardly be permanent.

No other Asian civilization exerted on Europe anything comparable to the attractive power of China. The interest of the
seventeenth century in Arabic studies meant that Muhammad-
anism was now ceasing to be feared and misunderstood as it
had been for centuries; but the Ottoman Empire, the one great
Moslem state with which Europeans had extensive contact,
seemed to deserve their contempt rather than their admiration.
A French translation of the *Zend-Avesta*, the sacred book of
the Zoroastrian religion, was published in 1771, and English
translations of the chief Hindu classics in the 1780s. Neither
Persia nor India, however, had any appreciable influence on the
intellectual life of Europe.

During the eighteenth century, then, Europe owed much to
her contacts with the rest of the world. Intercontinental trade
gave an important stimulus to her economic life and showed
far greater capacity for rapid growth than industry or agriculture. But this stimulus was very unevenly distributed. Trade
with America allowed the states of the Atlantic seaboard—

France, to some extent the Dutch Republic and Spain, above all Britain—to develop their economic and particularly their financial strength. Some of them could thus play in European affairs a role greater than they would otherwise have done. The gulf which separated the backward agrarian societies of east and central Europe from the more sophisticated and urbanized ones to be found in some parts of the west was growing wider as a result. The former, it now seemed to many contemporaries, were too poor to wage war unless they were subsidized by the latter; and, though this view was sometimes pushed too far, it was given colour by the subsidies which Britain paid to continental allies in the wars of the 1740s and 1750s with France and by the lavish expenditure of the French government on subsidies, bribes, and pensions in many European capitals. The European balance of power was slowly merging into a world, or at least an Atlantic, balance; this process heavily favoured those parts of the continent which possessed Atlantic coastlines, colonies, and large merchant marines. It correspondingly penalized those which did not have these advantages.

In the realm of ideas both China and the new United States of America exerted great influence, in quite different ways. Not until the twentieth century was European political thinking, in particular, to owe so much to non-European models. But these intellectual influences were soon to lose much of their impetus. After the 1760s the importance of China in this respect was in clear and rapid decline. The French Revolution deprived the American Revolution of its uniqueness and symbolic value in the eyes of European radicals. The two generations which followed saw European intellectual life once more turn in upon itself and largely ignore the outside world.

Nevertheless the eighteenth century gave birth to forces and problems which were to affect the relationship between Europe and the other continents for generations to come. It saw a very marked acceleration in the flow of emigrants to North America —not merely from the British Isles but also, an important pointer to the future, to some extent from other parts of Europe, notably west Germany. It saw a large volume of 'enlightened' criticism of slavery and the slave trade and the beginning, particularly in Britain, of a powerful movement for their abolition. It saw, side by side with much territorial aggressiveness and commercial greed in America, Africa, and Asia, a considerable movement of radical intellectual opinion against imperial expansion, notably where it involved, as in India or Spanish America, the subjection of a numerous native population. The Abbé Raynal's *Histoire . . . des établissements et du commerce des européens dans les deux Indes* (1770), one of the greatest best-sellers of the century, summed up a current of feeling of this kind which had been gathering strength for half a century or more, though it never succeeded in influencing the policies of governments. And even this suspicion and rejection of overseas expansion was itself an index of the influence of the outside world upon Europe.

# 7
# Conclusion

THE EVENTS OF 1789 in France, which now seem to mark so clearly the beginning of a new epoch in the history of Europe and the world—the meeting of the States-General in May, the fall of the Bastille in July, the forcible destruction of 'feudalism' by the spontaneous and unorganized peasant movement of the summer of that year—were not seen in this light by most contemporaries. To many of them the beginning of the revolution appeared as the more or less natural result of the position in which France found herself in the 1780s, and of her history during the eighteenth century.

This point of view was understandable and largely justified. What made the upheaval in France inevitable was the inability of the monarchy to control events, the incoherence and irrationality of the cumbersome administration, and above all the selfishness and irresponsibility of the privileged groups and institutions which bulked so large in the life of France as in much of the rest of Europe. The first of these factors was in part the result of the personal deficiencies of Louis XVI—well-meaning but weak, timid, and fundamentally ignorant of his people and their problems. But it was largely—and the second and third factors were entirely—the outcome of the way in which French life and government had been allowed to develop during past generations. The forces of privilege, the products of history and tradition, destroyed the old régime in France; by themselves radical ideas and even widespread popular suffering could not have achieved this. Into the breach which they made in the old structure of power there advanced, at first somewhat tentatively but soon irresistibly, the force of middle-class ambition and discontent. This, now revealed as the most dynamic and constructive element in French life, was itself the result of the economic and intellectual development of past decades and particularly of the last generation.

By 1786 the French government was in effect bankrupt; and the Contrôleur-Général des Finances, Calonne, proposed to raise the new revenue, which was now urgently needed, by means of a new land tax. This was to be levied uniformly and without exemptions. Moreover its collection was to be controlled by a system of new local assemblies whose members were to be drawn from all social orders. This, coupled with sharp cuts in government expenditure and a number of relatively minor reforms (notably an extension of the stamp duty), would, Calonne thought, allow the government to surmount its appalling financial difficulties. These were much more than merely financial proposals. The new land tax and its administration would undermine the existing structure of fiscal and political privilege in France; from this blow it could hardly hope to recover. Calonne's plans were therefore doomed to meet sustained opposition from the *parlements*, the hierarchy of the church, and much of the nobility. This opposition, allied with a widespread and largely unjustified popular fear of 'ministerial despotism' and of the overthrow of the structure of traditional rights which passed for a constitution in France, stultified them and opened the door to revolution.

The Assembly of Notables (officers of the *parlements* and the provincial estates, great nobles, church dignitaries, and government officials), which met early in 1787, turned down Calonne's proposals and won a good deal of public support in doing so. Early in April he was dismissed by Louis XVI, and his successor, Loménie de Brienne, attempted to force through a slightly modified version of his plans by destroying the power of the Parlement of Paris, whose members were exiled to Troyes. This effort to override privileged opposition to reform was even less successful than Calonne's more conciliatory policies. By the end of September the new land-tax had had to be withdrawn and the *parlement* had returned in triumph to the capital. In May 1788, after it had openly denounced the allegedly arbitrary government of the king and his ministers, the law courts were surrounded by troops, the leaders of the Parlement of Paris seized, and the powers of the *parlements* throughout France abolished by decree. The result was the virtual collapse of the authority of the government. The weakness of the monarchy, which had been growing for nearly three generations, was now clearly exposed to public view. The clergy and nobility supported the *parlements*, which also received widespread backing from public opinion. In many provincial cities rioting broke out and government officials were attacked; the collapse of public order which was to mark the whole course of the revolution was now under way. Once more the government, increasingly helpless, had to surrender. Brienne was replaced by Necker, who had been Contrôleur-Général in 1777–81 and who enjoyed a high and perhaps excessive reputation for ability and honesty. The *parlements* were recalled. Above all it was agreed that the States-General, the medieval representative body organized on a basis of social orders (Clergy, Nobility, and Third Estate) which had not met since 1614, should be summoned for May 1789. Its calling had been one of the main demands of the opponents of the government, and their only constructive one, ever since early in 1787.

Privileged conservatism seemed to have been completely victorious. Once more, as in the conflicts with the Parlement of Paris in 1720 and 1771–4, or in the great struggle over the proposals for new taxation in 1749–51 (see p. 93), the essential weakness of the monarchy and a lack of toughness and determination on the part of the ruler had been demonstrated. At the beginning of 1789 it was possible for some observers to believe that the outcome of the 'aristocratic revolt' of 1787–8 would be a further strengthening of the position and prerogatives of the privileged groups in French society. But these groups had now prepared the ground for genuine revolution. By the later months of 1788 and the early ones of 1789 the unprivileged but often educated and able members of the Third

Estate were increasingly beginning to feel themselves capable of playing a much greater part than hitherto, perhaps even a dominant part, in the government of France. By January 1789, in the most famous of all the hundreds of pamphlets produced during these months, Siéyès could claim that the Third Estate was the nation and that the privileged minority, a mere ex-crescence on the national life, had no rights that need be respected. Above all the disastrous food shortage and high prices produced by the bad harvests of 1787-8 were now gener-ating a spirit of genuinely popular revolution. Half-starved peasants and hungry and often unemployed workers in the towns were ready to attack the government and its agents, and above all the rights and claims of the landlords and the whole surviving structure of 'feudalism' in the French countryside. For a few months, and for the only time in the history of the revolution, the movement against the old régime was to become truly one of the masses.

It was the collapse of royal government in France in 1787-8 which was decisive in determining the direction of events. It meant that the old régime had been fatally weakened from within before the real revolution broke out at all. Yet there was nothing inevitable about this collapse. At the beginning of the century the French monarchy was without doubt the most powerful in Europe, the French administrative system in many ways a model to the rest of the continent. The history of eight-eenth-century France is littered with lost opportunities. If Louis XV and Louis XVI had been stronger and more intelli-gent men; if they had supported more effectively the able and reforming ministers at their disposal, such as Machault, Turgot, and Maupeou; if the pressures of tradition to engage in costly and prolonged wars had been less or had been resisted more effectively, the outcome could have been very different. The revolution was not caused merely by the near-famine condi-tions of the winter of 1788 and the spring and summer of 1789; the monarchy had survived more serious economic crises before. Still less was it produced by the spread of new social and poli-tical ideas, for these were accessible only to the educated and often of little effect even within that restricted circle. Of the

*cahiers de doléances*, the statements of grievances and proposals
for reform drawn up in hundreds all over France early in 1789
for the guidance of the States-General when it met, those of the
Third Estate show few traces of the thought or even of the
phraseology of the Enlightenment. Montesquieu is the only
major thinker of the century whose influence is visible in them.
Even in those of the clergy and nobility intellectual influence of
this kind is rare; and it must be remembered that the thought
of the Enlightenment was in general by no means hostile to
monarchy as an institution. The collapse of 1787–9 was the
result, not merely or even primarily of suffering and hope, but
of the history of France during the previous two or three generations, some aspects of which have been sketched in the preceding chapters. Above all it resulted from the failure to over-
come, even to face, the country's real problems, which marked
that history. Other great states—Russia, Spain, the Habsburg
Empire—had, in different ways, unsolved problems which were
even more serious than those of France. But in none of these
states were the forces of discontent so active, self-conscious,
and potentially powerful; and in none were the monarchy and
the existing political and social régime so weak and so fragile.

The immediate result as far as Europe was concerned of the
events of 1787–9 in France was her temporary weakening,
indeed nullification, as a factor in international relations. This
was very welcome to several of the powers. It made impossible
any French dominance of the Dutch Republic of the kind which
had been threatened for several years, and hence was very
gratifying to Prussia and above all to Great Britain. In September 1787 a Prussian army with British support destroyed the
power of the pro-French Patriot party in the Dutch provinces
and restored the authority of the Stadholder, William V, whose
wife was the sister of Frederick William II of Prussia. Above
all the collapse of the old régime meant that France could play
no active part in the new Russo-Turkish war which broke out
in August 1787.

This also had roots in the past. It sprang in part from
immediate grievances, notably from Turkish resentment at the

growth of Russian power in the Caucasus (where most of Georgia became a Russian protectorate in the summer of 1783). But behind these grievances was the fear and hatred which had been built up in Constantinople by a long history of conflict with Russia, and which had been brought to fever-pitch by the war of 1768–74 and the Russian seizure of the Crimea in 1783–4. From the outbreak of this new Russo-Turkish conflict there was to arise during the next three years the most complex international crisis which Europe had seen since the end of the Seven Years War. Much against his will, Joseph II, as the ally of Catherine of Russia since 1781, declared war on the Porte in February 1788. Gustavus III of Sweden, hoping to recover the Baltic territories lost to Russia in 1721, suddenly attacked her in July and signed an alliance and a subsidy treaty with the Turks a year later. The hostility of Prussia to the Habsburg Empire and of both Britain and Prussia to the ambitions of Catherine II ensured that by 1790–1 Europe was, for the first time for over a quarter of a century, in the grip of a crisis of continental and not merely of regional dimensions. Its outcome lies beyond the chronological limits of this book. Gustavus III made peace with Russia in August 1790, and Leopold II, the brother and successor of Joseph II, with the Turks in August 1791. Only in January 1792 did Catherine sign the Treaty of Jassy with the Turks. These complex struggles had none the less emphasized once more themes and problems already visible throughout the history of eighteenth-century Europe. The potentially vast power of Russia, now in many ways the greatest European state, had been again displayed; so had the vulnerability of the decaying Ottoman Empire; the weakness of the Habsburg territories as a result of their internal difficulties and exposed geographical position; and the bitterness of the Habsburg-Hohenzollern rivalry which Frederick II had set in motion when he invaded Silesia in 1740.

On the international level the history of Europe during the period covered by this book was dominated by war and territorial greed. The first decades of the century saw the forcible destruction of the European empires of Spain and Sweden, its

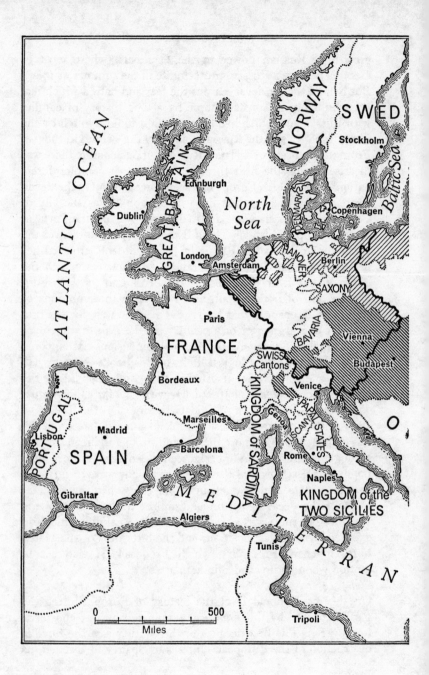

# Europe in 1789

Boundary of the Empire
Prussian Territory
Habsburg Territory

EN

St.Petersburg

Moscow

RUSSIA

POLAND

•Warsaw

Poltava

•Azov

•Jassy

Black Sea

Bucharest

Sofia

Constantinople

TTOMAN

Salonika

EMPIRE

• Aleppo

• Damascus

EAN SEA

REGMARAD

Alexandria

middle years the aggrandizement by war of Brandenburg-Prussia, and the 1760s and 1770s a new stage in the partition of the Ottoman Empire as well as the beginning of the end of Poland. For the first time the powers of Europe were effectively part of a single state-system, though one dominated by fear and greed to an extent hardly paralleled during most of the hundred years after 1815. Yet many of the major international developments which the eighteenth century saw—the striking growth of Russian power, the great expansion of the British empire, perhaps even the relative decline of France—might have been predicted in 1713 by an acute observer. Only the emergence of Brandenburg-Prussia as a state of the first or something near the first rank could not then have been foretold.

Within this increasingly unified system of states, social, economic, and administrative diversity between different areas of Europe, and even of the same state, were almost if not quite as great in 1789 as they had been at the death of Louis XIV. The struggles of enlightened despots, of reforming ministers, of innovating manufacturers and technologists, of radical thinkers and writers, were not in vain. But as yet the effect of their efforts, over most of the continent, had been little more than superficial. Genuine economic and social change, indeed, where it took place, often deepened and widened the gulf between different parts of Europe. As the Industrial Revolution developed in Britain in the last years of this period, and as it began faintly to affect France, the Austrian Netherlands, and a very few areas of Germany, it tended to throw into sharper contrast the economic and technological backwardness of eastern and much of central Europe. The same contrast is visible, though less clearly so, in the structure of society. Long before the Industrial Revolution began, the growth of towns, of trade, and to a lesser extent of financial organization, had produced in the more advanced areas of western Europe a movement, however slow and uncertain, towards a more modern type of society, one in which rank was based increasingly upon wealth. It was the impediments which this movement encountered in France, above all during the generation before 1789, which generated in the French bourgeoisie the potentially revolutionary temper that suddenly became visible in 1789. Over nearly the whole of central Europe, on the other hand, society remained traditional and even, if the word has any meaning, medieval. There it continued to be based on 'orders' and dominated more completely than in the west by landowners; while both Russia and the Ottoman Empire, in different ways, had by now developed societies peculiar to themselves which had little in common with those of western or even central Europe.

When the two or three generations before 1789 are considered as a whole the predominant impression which they leave on the observer is one of stability and resistance to change. Most Europeans in this period were closer to the thirteenth century than to the twentieth in their economic lives and social relationships. But this conservatism should not be exaggerated. In intellectual life above all there was change and growth. Sometimes, as in artistic, literary, and even political ideas, this growth was confused and lacking in clear lines of development. In other respects, however, notably in the physical sciences, it was consistent and cumulative. Above all it contributed two mutually incompatible elements to the century which followed: it laid the foundations of romanticism in literature, art, and political ideas, and it sowed the seed of the idea, potentially very dangerous to any *status quo*, that happiness can be, and ought to be, the normal condition of human life. Moreover the sudden acceleration of the pace of change, which is seen after about 1780, marks a turning-point in the history of Europe and of the world. In America there had been founded, in uniquely favourable conditions, a new independent state, of European origins but in some ways quite un-European. This state, contemporaries already saw, might in time overshadow those of Europe. Modern industrialism, which could not be confined for long to its original homeland in Britain, was beginning to change the life of the ordinary man, though this was as yet hardly visible, more radically than anything since Neolithic times. The dissemination of ideas through the printed word was assuming hitherto unknown proportions; something like a modern public opinion was beginning to be possible in a few parts of Europe, with all that this implied for political life, both within the states and internationally.

We are still far from the modern world in 1789. A Europe in which society was still almost everywhere so fragmented and so traditional, a Europe without mass literacy or mass armies, or the idea, except in the writings of a very few visionaries, of any mass participation in politics, was remote indeed from that of the present day. Yet it was part of the soil from which the modern world grew; and with the outbreak of the revolution in France that growth became unmistakable.

# Bibliography

The list which follows, it scarcely needs to be said, is incomplete and selective. It is merely an attempt to indicate to the reader some of the more important books and very occasionally articles, in west European languages, in which he may pursue further different aspects of the subject. A very useful and much fuller guide to reading can be found in J. S. Bromley and A. Goodwin, *A Select List of Works on Europe and Europe Overseas, 1715–1815* (Oxford, 1956).

The best detailed discussion of eighteenth-century Europe is now that supplied by the two relevant volumes of the New Cambridge Modern History. These are: Vol. VII, *The Old Régime, 1713–1763*, ed. J. O. Lindsay (Cambridge, 1957) and Vol. VIII, *The American and French Revolutions, 1763–1793*, ed. A. Goodwin (Cambridge, 1965). There are also three volumes, of somewhat varying merit, to be noted in the Rise of Modern Europe series edited by W. L. Langer: P. Roberts, *The Quest for Security, 1715–40* (New York–London, 1947); W. L. Dorn, *Competition for Empire, 1740–63* (London–New York, 1940); and L. Gershoy, *From Despotism to Revolution, 1763–89* (New York–London, 1944). In French there is E. Préclin and V. L. Tapié, *Le XVIIIᵉ siècle* (Paris, 1952), which makes up Vol. VII Parts ii and iii of the series Clio: Introduction aux Études Historiques; it contains a vast amount of information and very large bibliographies. There are also two relevant volumes in the French series Peuples et Civilisations: P. Muret, *La Prépondérance anglaise, 1713–1763* (Paris, 1937) and P. Sagnac, *La Fin de l'ancien régime et la révolution américaine, 1763–1789* (Paris, 1941). R. Mousnier and E. Labrousse, *Le XVIIIᵉ siècle: Révolution intellectuelle, technique et politique, 1715–1815* (Paris, 1953) is particularly good on some aspects of social and intellectual life. The most recent large-scale German treatment is *Von der Reformation zur Revolution* (Berlin–Frankfurt–Vienna, 1964) which is Vol. VII of G. Mann and A. Nitschke (eds.), Propyläen Weltgeschichte: Eine Universalgeschichte.

The best histories of Great Britain for this period are the two relevant volumes in the Oxford History of England series: B. Williams, *The Whig Supremacy, 1714–60* (2nd ed., Oxford, 1962); and J. Steven Watson, *The Reign of George III, 1760–1815* (Oxford, 1960). Both are equipped with very large and up-to-date bibliographies. For France the best recent book is J. Lough, *An Introduction to Eighteenth-Century France* (London, 1960). On the Habsburg Empire there are H. Hantsch, *Die Geschichte Oesterreichs*, Vol. II (Vienna, 1950) and H. Marczali, *Hungary in the Eighteenth Century* (Cambridge, 1910). For Prussia O. Hintze, *Die Hohenzollern und ihr Werk* (Berlin, 1916) is still in some ways the best account. V. Gitermann, *Geschichte Russlands* (Zürich, 1944–49) Vol. II is now the most useful account of eighteenth-century Russia in a western language, and Vols. V and VI of A. Ballesteros y Beretta, *Historia de Espana y de su influencia en la historia universal* (Barcelona, 1918–41) are a standard account of eighteenth-century Spain. F. Valsecchi, *L'Italia nel settecento* (Milan, 1959) is up to date and lavishly illustrated.

On the history of international relations during this period the best single book is undoubtedly G. Zeller, *Les temps modernes*, ii: *De Louis XIV à 1789* (Paris, 1955), which forms part of the series Histoire des Relations Internationales edited by P. Renouvin. Important works on special topics, arranged roughly in chronological order of their subjects are: R. Wittram, *Peter I, Czar und Kaiser* (Göttingen, 1964), which contains an excellent account of the diplomacy of the Great Northern War; A. Baudrillart, *Philippe V et la cour de France* (Paris, 1890–1900) Vols. III–V; A. McC. Wilson, *French Foreign Policy during the Administration of Cardinal Fleury* (Cambridge, Mass., 1936); R. Pares, *War and Trade in the West Indies, 1739–1763* (Oxford, 1936)—a brilliant study of Anglo-French rivalry in an area crucial to both combatants—and the same author's 'American versus Continental Warfare, 1739–1763', *English Historical Review* LI (1936). R. Waddington, *Louis XV et le renversement des alliances, 1754–56* (Paris, 1896) is still the standard large-scale treatment of the 'Diplomatic Revolution', and the same author's unfinished *La guerre de sept ans* (Paris, 1896–1914) contains a vast amount of information. A. Sorel, *The Eastern Question in the*

*Eighteenth Century* (London, 1898) is still useful; and H. Uebersberger, *Russlands Orientpolitik in den letzten zwei Jahrhunderten* Vol. I (Stuttgart, 1913) is fundamental to its subject though thin on the 1780s and early 1790s. H. H. Kaplan, *The First Partition of Poland* (New York, 1962) is the most complete English account of its subject. The international aspects of the revolt of Britain's American colonies are well covered in S. F. Bemis, *The Diplomacy of the American Revolution* (New York, 1935) and the Dutch crisis of 1787 in A. Cobban, *Ambassadors and Secret Agents* (London, 1954).

There is no adequate study of European society as a whole during this period; perhaps it would be impossible to write one. However A. Goodwin (ed.), *The European Nobility in the Eighteenth Century* (London, 1953) is a very useful collection of essays, and D. Gerhard, 'Regionalismus und ständisches Wesen als ein Grundthema europäischer Geschichte', *Historische Zeitschrift* CLXXIV (1952) is an article of great penetration. R. R. Palmer, *The Age of the Democratic Revolution* Vol. I (Princeton, 1959) throws much light on the interrelations of society and political life in the generation 1760–90. On separate countries there are P. Sagnac, *La Formation de la société française moderne* (Paris, 1945–46); A. Dominguez Ortiz, *La sociedad espanola en el siglo XVIII* (Madrid, 1955); and M. Berengo, *La società veneta alla fine del settecento* (Florence, 1956).

On the economic history of Europe two good general books are J. M. Kulischer, *Allgemeine Wirtschaftsgeschichte* Vol. II (Munich–Berlin, 1929) and H. Heaton, *An Economic History of Europe* (London, 1948). T. S. Ashton, *The Industrial Revolution, 1760 to 1830* (London, 1948) is an excellent short treatment of its subject; the same author's *An Economic History of England: the Eighteenth Century* (London, 1955) is also very good; and P. Mantoux, *The Industrial Revolution in the Eighteenth Century* (12th ed. London, 1961) is still the most detailed general treatment of its subject. Phyllis Deane, *The First Industrial Revolution* (Cambridge, 1965) is more technical but very useful. E. F. Hecksher, *An Economic History of Sweden* (Cambridge, Mass., 1954) and F. Lütge, *Deutsche Sozial- und Wirtschaftsgeschichte* (Berlin–Göttingen–Heidelberg, 1952) are good recent general studies of other parts of Europe. Much work is still being done on the problems of population-growth; here J. T. Krause, 'Some Implications of Recent Work in Historical Demography', *Comparative Studies in Society and History* I (1958–9) is useful. H. Sée, *Esquisse d'une histoire du régime agraire en Europe aux XVIIIᵉ et XIXᵉ siècles* (Paris, 1921) is one of the few attempts at a general study of agrarian history, though it does not cover eastern Europe. Other important aspects of economic life are treated on a supra-national scale in J. Lacour-Gayet (ed.), *Histoire du commerce* (Paris, 1950–5), Vol. IV; J. G. Van Dillen (ed.), *The History of the Principal Public Banks* (The Hague, 1934); and C. Singer and others (eds.), *A History of Technology* (Oxford, 1954–8), Vols. III–IV.

On problems of government the book by R. R. Palmer mentioned above is almost the only important one on more than a national scale; the Historical Association pamphlet on *Enlightened Despotism* by F. Hartung (London, 1957) is useful though short. Some of the more important studies of individual rulers or states are: R. Pares, *King George III and the Politicians* (Oxford, 1953); P. von Mitrofanov, *Joseph II: Seine politische und kulturelle Tätigkeit* (Vienna–Leipzig, 1910); F. Fejtö, *Un Habsbourg révolutionnaire, Joseph II* (Paris, 1953); F. Valsecchi, *L'Assolutismo illuminato in Austria e in Lombardia* (Bologna, 1931); D. Dakin, *Turgot and the Ancien Régime in France* (London, 1939); and R. A. Dorwart, *The Administrative Reforms of Frederick William I of Prussia* (Cambridge, Mass., 1953).

Intellectual and cultural life is so vast and complex a subject that only the most arbitrary and summary suggestions for reading can be given. The history of science is covered by A. R. Hall, *The Scientific Revolution, 1500–1800* (London, 1954) and in greater detail in A. Wolf, *A History of Science, Philosophy, and Technology in the Eighteenth Century* (2nd ed., London, 1952). On political ideas and their background the best single volumes are perhaps P. Hazard, *European Thought in the Eighteenth Century: from Montesquieu to Lessing* (London, 1954) and A. Cobban, *In Search of Humanity* (London, 1960), while P. Gay, *The Party of Humanity: Studies in the French Enlightenment* (London, 1964) is very stimulating. There is an excellent biography of Montesquieu by R. Shackleton (Oxford, 1961), and on Rousseau's personality there is an interesting book by R. Grimsley, *Jean-Jacques Rousseau: a Study in Self-Awareness* (Cardiff, 1961). The most important recent work on Rousseau's political ideas is R. Derathé, *J.-J. Rousseau et la science politique de son temps* (Paris, 1950). The best general work on the Catholic church is E. Préclin and E. Jarry, *Les luttes politiques et doctrinales aux XVIIᵉ et XVIIIᵉ siècles*, Part ii (Paris, 1956), which makes up Vol. XIX of the series Histoire de l'Église depuis les Origines jusqu'à nos Jours, while R. R. Palmer, *Catholics and Unbelievers in Eighteenth-Century France* (Princeton, 1939) is of importance from more than a religious point of view. A. Gazier, *Histoire générale du mouvement janséniste* (Paris, 1922) is a standard work on its subject. On the history of art P. Lavedan, *Histoire de l'art* Vol. II (Paris, 1944) is a good general treatment with full bibliographies, and R. Wellek, *A History of Modern Criticism, 1750–1950* Vol. I (London, 1955) is excellent on the development of literary ideas. On music P. H. Lang, *Music in Western Civilization* (New York, 1941) is a good general survey.

The history of the major European colonial empires can be followed in the Cambridge History of the British Empire Vol. I (Cambridge, 1929); J. Saintoyant, *La colonisation française sous l'ancien régime* Vol. II (Paris, 1929); C. H. Haring, *The Spanish Empire in America* (New York, 1947); and C. de Lannoy and H. Van der Linden, *Histoire de l'expansion coloniale des peuples européens*, 2 vols. (Paris–Brussels, 1907–11); this does not cover the British or French empires. K. E. Knorr, *British Colonial Theories, 1570–1850* (Toronto, 1944) gives many references to the very plentiful contemporary pamphlet material. E. E. Williams, *Capitalism and Slavery* (Chapel Hill, 1944) and H. Furber, *John Company at Work* (Cambridge, Mass., 1948) throw light on the economic aspects of imperial expansion in the eighteenth century. H. Honour, *Chinoiserie: the Vision of Cathay* (London, 1961); W. W. Appleton, *A Cycle of Cathay* (New York, 1951); and B. Guy, *The French Image of China before and after Voltaire* (Geneva, 1963) throw light on the rise and fall of Chinese artistic and intellectual influences in eighteenth-century Europe.

# Index